T0279639

LOST MILLS
of
FULTON COUNTY

LISA M. RUSSELL

THE
History
PRESS

Published by The History Press
Charleston, SC
www.historypress.com

First published 2023

Manufactured in the United States

ISBN 9781467153584

Library of Congress Control Number: 2022948307

For the Russell men in my life:
David, John, Michael, Samuel, and Wheeler David

CONTENTS

LOST THINGS

In 2015, I lost my Luke Skywalker. The pain is still—*sniffle*—palpable. Understand that this was no ordinary Luke. My loving parents gave him to me—along with his iconic Sand Speeder and X-Wing—in 1977, the year when *Star Wars* changed the world. He was an original and mine and completely irreplaceable. At ten years old, I understood his value, not in dollars and cents but in the special place he'd always hold in my life. I cared deeply for him, even as he became just one of the many *Star Wars* figurines I would collect. He'd forever be my Number One; nothing could separate us. I had planned to be buried with him.

So, how and why did a middle-aged man lose his beloved toy? (There are so many things wrong with that question, but here we are.) Despite my wife Nina's admonishment, Luke accompanied me to see *The Force Awakens*. How could I deny him the chance to witness his long-awaited future finally coming to pass? Well, Nina wasted her breath. Although she recognized the inherent dangers of taking a small toy into a dark and crowded theater rife with grabby-little-children fingers, I—being older and, thus, wiser—in no uncertain terms let her talk to the hand. Not only would Luke attend the film, but he would receive a VIP view of the screen in my seat's cupholder, which of course, depending on a person's perspective, was also someone else's cupholder.

In my full-grown-man mind, everything was under control. Luke was inextricably part of my past; there was no way he wouldn't be in my future. Well, Luke totally Force Ghosted me, and I have only myself to blame (as Nina will gleefully attest). Even worse, I honestly have no idea what happened. I'd like to believe that an evil child stole him, yet when I wrack my brain, a part of me thinks that I simply forgot him. Suffering from post-movie *Star Wars* Fan-Boy fever, I probably left Luke behind…alone in the cupholder…like a discarded Twizzlers wrapper. Oh, the humanity.

Speaking of humanity—everyone everywhere has a tendency to lose things. It's an all-too-common trait that transcends age, ethnicity, religion, sex, politics—you name it. This said, I propose there are three Lost Things categories that define, in order of severity, how humans lose…things. In the least unfavorable instance, there's no shame: a person loses something unintentionally and without doing something totally stupid. It just happens. This is the "Oopsie Daisy!" category. Usually, it's small objects, like car keys, coins, the bar napkin with a hottie's digits, that one sock, your marbles, etc. Or sometimes it's a huge thing, like the Continent of Atlantis. While it's pretty frustrating, we can find a legitimate excuse: darn shallow pockets, he distracted me, it rolled down the sewer, gremlins, it was an act of god (pick a god). And if you carefully search the recesses of your couch, dig far enough into the earth's crust, or check inside that superfluous, tiny inside pocket of your pants, these items might turn up again. No harm, no foul.

Then again, sometimes arrogance, complacency, or just lousy judgment lead people to lose things. This is the "Mea Culpa!" category—when we should have known better, paid attention, and listened to the voices that cautioned us to reconsider. Losing these things makes a person kick himself (often in my case) or get kicked (also often in my case). These items are permanently lost because of bad choices, like schlepping your beloved Luke to the movies; letting your sister's indoor cat outside; loaning money to an artist friend; flying a box kite in a hurricane; putting off roof repairs even though families of raccoons, squirrels, and possibly pterosaurs have made nests inside of it; and so on. Fortunately, there is one saving grace for people who unadvisedly dabble in "Mea Culpa!": although the objects are lost forever, losing them was still unintended, which is convenient for anyone with a guilty conscience.

Last is the potentially nefarious "Just Get Rid of It!" category, which contains acts of irretrievably destructive loss. Such loss can be callously and unrepentantly wanton (due to spite, fear, anger, greed, etc.) or at times caused by a false sense of progress (due to ignorance, lack of imagination, peer pressure, half a brain, etc.). Not to be judgy, but the people who truly excel in this category, intentionally ridding the world of all sorts of fantastic stuff, should never be forgiven (okay, I'm judgy). The "Just Get Rid of It" humans typically reek of egocentrism and crow that they are creating some sort of utopia (I call BS). They blow up giant Buddhas, melt down ancient relics, burn books and priceless art, and bulldoze someone else's history. They myopically only see the Here and Now, devaluing the Past. But hey, before this section gets too preachy, I should mention that not all people who fit into the "Just Get Rid of It" category are wicked tyrants hell-bent on the self-serving ruination or reinterpretation of the world. In fact, my Peter Panism dogma dictates that someone tossing out a perfectly good toy also falls into this category—it's an absolutely senseless loss that made Pixar executives boo-coo moolah and that I would never allow in a million years, much to my wife's chagrin.

Speaking of wives—in 2016, Nina and I founded The Patch Works Art & History Center to push back as hard as our little idealistic hearts could against all three Lost Things categories, especially against the "Just Get Rid of It!" attitude that continues to pervade Atlanta, which has been universally ridiculed for destroying any structure older than twenty years. Atlanta is awesome, but preserving its historic buildings and communities can feel like storming Mordor. We might ultimately prevail, but first, we're gonna have to battle a heckuva lotta nasty and ill-tempered denizens.

As Nina and I have delved further into the world of historic preservation, we've come to learn that oftentimes allegedly "lost" history can be hiding in plain sight. It's alive and kicking but simply on hiatus. It didn't fall unluckily out of someone's pocket, get mindlessly left behind, or get mercilessly obliterated; it's just patiently waiting.

Nina and I spend gobs of energy being history sleuths, piecing together scattered fragments of Lost Things. We follow faint clues leading us down multi-forking trails of memories until we finally discover a comprehensive narrative, eventually presenting a reconstituted history to the public. Sure, we mine the usual resources—dusty old tomes, brown and tattered newspaper articles, deathly quiet and eerily lit archives, and so on—but we also uncover vast amounts of history lurking in the intangible recollections of our neighbors and in atypical objects such as an antique love letter or a tombstone, much of which can be found in our figurative backyard. Next time you walk down a street, look around and consider that even a seemingly mundane landscape holds stories that are chock-full of human experiences.

When Lisa Russell contacted us, we immediately recognized a kindred spirit. She sees Lost Things all around her. While others may remain steadfastly disinterested in the Past, she relishes solving the conundrums of the forgotten-but-not-gone world. She meticulously performs the research and publishes her findings as accessible, unpretentious, and entertaining books (who says history has to be boring?). Of course, we also really dig that she's been focusing on Georgia. We ain't at all biased. Nope.

Her newest opus, *Lost Mills of Fulton County*, delves into a topic that is dear to Nina's and my collective heart. Our family built and ran a successful cotton mill located right smack dab in Atlanta (and for those who don't know, Atlanta is in Fulton County; Fulton County is not in Atlanta). Although Fulton Bag and Cotton Mills stopped operating long ago, it has nonetheless survived after being rehabilitated and converted into lofts. Other, less fortunate Fulton County mills have sadly vanished. But Lisa can tell you more about that in her book.

In conclusion, Lisa fearlessly takes on the daunting task of chronicling Lost Things. Her efforts demonstrate that how something gets lost doesn't matter. What matters is that someone is willing to tell the stories. While the tangible remains of a historic structure are nifty, they are only the precursor to a much larger endeavor: the detective work. Lisa seeks the elusive intangibles and solves Lost Things mysteries. She reaches out, grabs those puzzle pieces, and puts them together. I can say from experience that this is no easy thing. We at The Patch Works applaud her love of history. Lisa's books are a testament to how, when someone puts in the time, something once thought lost can be recovered. So yes, my Luke Skywalker may be gone, but you now know his story. His history will exist forever.

—Jacob Elsas

Jacob Elsas is the great-great-grandson of a nineteenth-century German-speaking Jewish immigrant—his namesake, Jacob Elsas. In 1881, Jacob founded Fulton Bag and Cotton Mills (née Fulton Cotton Spinning Company). For decades, the mill was one of the country's leaders in cotton bag production. But like most textile companies in the 1970s, changes in consumer demands and a crippling recession damaged the industry.

In 1981, the factory finally closed its doors. The mill buildings remained abandoned, falling into disrepair, and facing an uncertain future. In the early 1990s, the Cabbagetown-based Save the Mill movement prompted a large-scale adaptive-reuse project. The movement rehabilitated the dilapidated structures, converting the mill into residential lofts.

Today, Fulton Cotton Mill Lofts is the only intact example of Fulton County's once-prosperous cotton mill industry. In 2016, Jacob and his wife, Nina, opened the Patch Works Art and History Center to preserve and tell stories. Jake and Nina tell the good, the bad, and the ugly truths about the historic cotton mill and its mill town, now known as Cabbagetown. To learn more about their work, please visit thepatchworks.org.

PREFACE

I left much unsaid. While writing my third book, *Lost Mill Towns of North Georgia*, I ran out of word count. When I reached forty-five thousand words, I had to cut. Unfortunately, Fulton County had to go. I put a lot of research aside and thought, "Maybe later." Later happens in this volume.

Fulton County mills have a character and creation different from their northern neighbors. Both Fulton County and North Georgia are part of the Piedmont. According to the New Georgia Encyclopedia, the Georgia Piedmont lies between the Blue Ridge Mountains and the Upper Coastal Plain. Golley says, "It runs in a northeast-to-southwest direction, following the main axis of the mountains, faults, and coastline of the southeastern United States."[1]

The northern mills grew communities that bred paternalism. In an urban location, the Fulton County mills had less caring and more controlling owners. The Fulton County workforce came from the same hills that filled the North Georgia mills. When the farm could no longer support them, workers came to the mills. Some stayed in the northern counties, and some migrated farther south to Fulton. The workforce in the city was fluid. Instability opened the door to union invasions and strikes in 1914 and 1934. North Georgia mills had strikes, but they were more like a family.[2]

Industrial scholars studied this region as the cotton belt and the new industrial South. While a few cotton mills existed before the Civil War, Reconstruction brought mills to the cotton fields; the cotton mill era was born.

Industrial scholars like Gary Fink and Clifford Kuhn left invaluable research. Fink pulled the espionage records from the basement of Fulton

Bag and Cotton. Kuhn went out and interviewed the workers of Exposition for firsthand accounts. Their work explaining the mills in Fulton County is foundational. I offer another perspective.

I have written three books about lost places in Georgia. When I go to speak near those lost towns, sometimes the locals get offended. "What do you mean, lost? We are not lost; we are still here."

True, some of the lost towns still exist. But the essence of the place has changed, and the original purpose is gone. These communities are full of ghosts and shadows. Fulton County mills differ from North Georgia mills in that very little remains. The cotton mill in Lindale, Georgia, is a wedding venue. Canton Mills renovated the old buildings into lofts and retail space. Only Fulton Bag and Cotton resurrected its lofts.

Roswell Mill Park is a popular outdoor space. The walking trails and a rebuilt covered bridge give a feel for what once was. The 1882 mill is an event space, yet the original pre–Civil War mill buildings have long since crumbled into the red dirt. Along the banks of Vickery (Big) Creek, a trail leads to the old mill wheels and the falls that powered the mill.

In northeast Atlanta, an oasis from urban sprawl is a town once called Chattahoochee, now part of Fulton County. Whittier Mill Village remains a vibrant community. They preserve their past with a park where the old mill walls stand as a reminder of the 1896 mill.

We lost the Atlanta Cotton Factory and Exposition Mill buildings to history. Henry Grady pushed H.I. Kimball to usher in the New South by opening the first cotton mill in Atlanta, the Atlanta Cotton Factory. With limited success, the factory did not survive. Other mills thrived. Exposition Mills was born in the 1881 Cotton Exposition. After the fair closed, the mill opened using the Exposition buildings. After a good run, the mill disappeared from the Atlanta landscape. They paved over the mill, while the mill village remained.

Fulton Bag and Cotton is the only surviving cotton mill building in Fulton County. Today, it contains luxury lofts in a gated community. Outside the gates is Cabbagetown, the former mill village. It is a neighborhood of artists living in preserved homes. This former mill town has found a new life.

This book attempts to take readers back to the old mills of Fulton County. Tour these haunted places and meet the people who made lives in the villages. Honor these places and remember those who built these places to profit from textiles.

We live in a rootless world. Too much of metro Atlanta's history has been bulldozed. Even large cities like Atlanta and prominent counties like Fulton must protect their roots. So much is already gone, and many uprooted memories leave us unstable. We need stability.

In my search, I found a few communities still rooted in their past. The three mill towns that cling to their history have found a purpose in their place. The two lost mills have lived only in archives. Until now.

Fulton Mills and their villages come to life in *Lost Mills of Fulton County*.

Acknowledgements

An old Baptist preacher once told me that while he prepared his sermons, "I milk a lot of cows but churn my own butter." Thank you, Reverend Oscar Michael, for your in-depth scholarship and skillful research.

When writing these books, I must stand on the shoulders of giants. Researchers who came before allowed me to climb on piles of primary sources. Without their help, my task would be impossible.

The industrial scholars anchored my searches for the lost Fulton mills. See the bibliography for complete information on the works of Gary Fink, Clifford M. Kuhn, Michael D. Hitt, Franklin M. Garrett, Jacquelyn D. Hall, Mary D. Petite, Douglas A. Blackmon, and Ruth B. Cook. These scholars dug deep and pulled out so much history. I hope this book will complement their work.

Two men I met along this journey were so committed to telling Fulton mill village narratives. Jacob "Jake" Elsas added a province to the Fulton Bag and Cotton Company story. He also helps to keep Cabbagetown alive through the Patch. Thank you for opening this book with your insightful foreword.

A passionate historian, Donald Rooney loves his home—the Whittier Mill Village. The Whittier Mill Village Association preserves its history while caring about the community. They maintain a directory, web page, and park; they rescued the mill ruins before it was too late. Whittier Mill Village Association supports the reclamation of Chattahoochee Brick Company for good.

Without our local historical societies, we would have lost so many artifacts. Thank you, Elaine Deniro from Roswell History Center. Your generosity began my research for this book.

I had to visit the Kenan Research Center at the Atlanta History Center to experience the magic. Staci Catron and her staff diligently pulled box after box for my search. I look forward to working with them on my next title of Georgia history.

At the Georgia Tech Archives, I touched a last bag off the production line of Fulton Bag. My appreciation to Katie Gentilello; she went beyond to help me find the facts I needed.

I did not visit Georgia State University, but its digital collection for labor studies is deep and wide.

On a personal note, I am dedicating this book to the Russell men in my life, including my three sons, John, Michael, and Samuel. Samuel and John have gone to great lengths to help me with my research. Thank you to my husband of almost forty years, John David, for putting up with the trips and hours of writing. And welcome to the world, Wheeler David Russell. You were born while I was writing in the waiting room. I hope the royalties will give you pocket change someday.

Not to leave out the corresponding Russell women who make this family work: Laura Leigh, Becka, and Elisabeth. Thank you for putting up with my sons and giving me my granddaughters, Charlotte, Louisa, and Josie.

I need lots of encouragement. I am insecure and needy. My colleague and friend Jennifer Dixon has kept me healthy with her potions so I can live to write another day. Dr. Jodie Vangrov, you are still the best boss ever. My writing career might have stopped if not for your encouragement.

Friends come and go. Some come for a season and others for a reason. Some friends stay for a lifetime. Ella Landrum, you are all three. Amy Grant sings it best: "If you find someone who's faithful and find someone who's true—thank the Lord, He's been doubly good to you."

After COVID-19 harassed us, I tried to reconnect with people who have been dear to me. Two special ones became more special after years of disconnection from my life. Rita Bell, you are a beautiful free spirit; I am proud of your life journey. Nicey T. Eller, thank you for reconnecting after forty years. You inspire me still.

To The History Press: I had always loved your books—long before I wrote one for you. Thank you to my patient editor, Joe Gartrell. The opportunities they have given me are invaluable. I look forward to more titles with my favorite editor and publisher.

INTRODUCTION

Fulton County was once a robust cotton capital. Cotton was king for decades. Before the Civil War, few Georgia cotton mills were prospering. With Reconstruction, men like Henry Grady pressed for a New South economy—especially in Fulton County. New cotton mills popped up in the city after a series of expositions: the 1881 International Cotton Exposition, the 1887 Piedmont Exposition, and the highly marketed 1895 Cotton States and International Exposition.

Georgia history and southern American history intersect with the Fulton Mills story. The book is about the pre–Civil War period. Legacy is strong. This story involves race, reconstruction, New South ideology, labor relations, southern industrial history, and socioeconomic evolution. These stories are about people and places. The men, women, and children of the mills have their own voices. The purpose of the mills has changed. Some mill locations have disappeared into urban creep. The original Fulton County mills are gone but not forgotten. The tendrils of this early turn-of-the-twentieth-century mill era grow deep into southern culture and Atlanta's story today.

An old brochure promotes a great fair. The 1895 *Official Guide to Atlanta, Including Information of the Cotton State and International Exposition* explains in flowery language why Atlanta and Fulton County are the perfect place and time for the Fulton mill era:

> *Early in the nineteenth century nature reigned supreme among the chincapin woods that densely covered the rolling slopes of the Piedmont hills in this locality.*

The stillness was unbroken save by the songs of birds and the babbling of waters that found their sources among the hundred springs that are now embraced within the city's limit. The winds held high carnival, wild and free, above the sultry breezes in the valleys, a thousand feet below.

Margaret Severance wrote the official guide to Fulton County, Georgia, in 1895. Her prose is flowery:

The Cherokee and Choctaw Indians, and later the white hunter, frequently startled the wild deer from this favorite resort. Here nature had formed a gateway that was recognized and made use of by these fleet animals before its advantages were recognized by man. When pursed by the hunter up the Chattahoochee or Okmulgee rivers at this point, the frightened animals would bound across the country to the river on either side and escape by the aid of the rapid-flowing stream.

In 1828, miners flocked to this region in search of gold. Henry Ivy was the first white man that preferred a home in this locality.

Later a few families settled here, and in 1836 there was nestled among the woods a straggling settlement, the infant queen of which we boast to day, but so modest and obscure that she hardly dare to won a name. Surrounded on every side, cradled, and protected by her own forests, Atlanta knew nothing of the outer world.[3]

In this marketing document, she explained the expulsion of the Native Americans from Georgia in an unapologetic tone:

Soon after the country began to be settled by the whites there arose between the Cherokee Indians and the State of Georgia a dispute concerning the overlap claims. Boundary lines were indefinite. After considerable difficulty the Indians were persuaded to accept certain terms and be removed west of the Mississippi river. In 1839 this was accomplished. The best possible means was provided for their transportation, and those that refused to go were taken by force. The Cherokees held a treaty with the United States Government. Their claims interfering with the rights of the State of Georgia.[4]

Margaret Severance wrote this brochure in the latter days of Reconstruction to promote the 1895 Cotton Exposition. Strangely, this marketing document continues laying out how Atlanta developed into a transportation hub, ignoring slavery and the Civil War:

Augusta, Macon, and Columbus were the landing places of this section. The people carried their ginseng, cotton, hams, etc., to these places and exchanged them for coffee, sugar, and various products brought to the landing places for distribution. Only hoofed animals were used. But little money was in circulation at that time. Commerce consisted chiefly of exchange.

What was then considered the great Northwest is now known as Kentucky, Ohio, Indiana, and Illinois. That country looked steadfastly to the South for an outlet for its products. Charleston and Savannah were leading ports. At the discovery of the great use of steam, the heart of Georgia throbbed and longed to reach out to the world.

The remaining history of our city is necessarily an account of its railroads. Charleston and Augusta were connected by rail. Meetings were held by leading men of this country at Knoxville and various other places to consider the best route to join the great Northwest with Charleston and Savannah. The Western & Atlantic Railroad was built by the State of Georgia in 1843.

The surveyors were instructed to lay the road to the most convenient geographical position. They surveyed the land to the point on which the Union Depot now stands, a few roads south of where the principal crossroads of these hills intersected. These roads were known as the Marietta, Peachtree, Whitehall, and Decatur roads and still retain these names as main streets. This place was then conveniently called Terminus, the end of the Western & Atlantic Railroad.

The first engine ever seen here was known as the "Florida." It was brought from Madison by sixteen mules. Madison was, at that time, the flourishing terminus of the Georgia Railroad. The people gathered around the country to behold the strange and almost living thing. The Indian war-whoop had died away. Progress, courage and enterprise possessed the people and had come to stay. In 1815, the Georgia Railroad was completed from Madison to Terminus, which had taken the name of Marthasville, now Atlanta. The first through train from Augusta was conducted by Col. G.W. Adair, one of our oldest and most respected citizens. Thus, the leading ports of the South, Charleston and Savannah, were connected at this point by rail, with the great Northwest. The Georgia Railroad from the East and the Western & Atlantic from the North.

This brought high hopes and great claims for Marthasville, as the great Northwest had an outlet for her products and all transportation was to be brought through the Gate City. Real estate sold at public auction. Schools, newspapers, and churches were founded, and Marthasville absorbed

*the country towns and villages about her. She was constantly receiving
tributes. Country boys aspired to a profession or trade sought this center for
opportunities. The next railroad completed to Marthasville was the Macon
& Western, after which this city became a distributing point.*

*In 1852, the Atlanta & West Point Railroad came from the West. And
thus, it was that Atlanta's first roads were established, and on through time,
it has never lost an opportunity to advance.*[5]

Then there was a war. The Civil War tore up this perfect plan. Union
soldiers tore up those railroads and tied Sherman's bow ties with bent rails.
While Atlanta burned, entrepreneurs like H.I. Kimball and Jacob Elsas
came to town to rebuild not for altruism but for personal fortune. Henry
Grady, a newspaperman who became famous for his New South ideas to
bring the cotton factories to the cotton fields in Georgia, encouraged them.

In 1879, Kimball built the first cotton factory in Atlanta. The following
year, Elsas, already a successful businessperson, bought a charter from
Kimball to open the later-named Fulton Bag and Cotton Company. The
year after the 1881 Exposition, the location was used to open Exposition
Mills. While Roswell Manufacturing Company existed since 1839, Federal
troops burned the mills under Sherman's orders in July 1864. The board of
directors rebuilt the mills, and they prospered during Reconstruction. After
the 1895 Exposition, Whittier Mills came south and built a mill and a village
in northeast Atlanta.

I always start with, "Why?" "Who cares?" is my primary research question
when writing about lost things. Why do we need to remember the lost mills
of Fulton County? We examine the legacy of hard work, strikes, labor unions,
and the origin of Labor Day in a post-COVID-19 world that infected our work
ethic. Hiring people to work in your homes or mow grass is nearly impossible.
No one wants to work. The new term *quiet quitting* is an age-old concept of
laziness. In the textile mill era, quiet quitting would have led to loud firing. I
teach technical college students. I encourage students to do their best daily to
build infrastructure and make more money than their instructors. Still, it is a
struggle to pull them along. A failing economy may give rise to a revived work
ethic like the mill era, with better pay and a better life.

Knowing the history of lost things is essential because it gives a solid
foundation for the next generation. My father was a hard worker. He did
not have the benefits of even a technical education. Still, he taught himself,
worked hard and then retired after years of managing mills and inventing
new machinery. He was never rich, but he left a work ethic legacy.

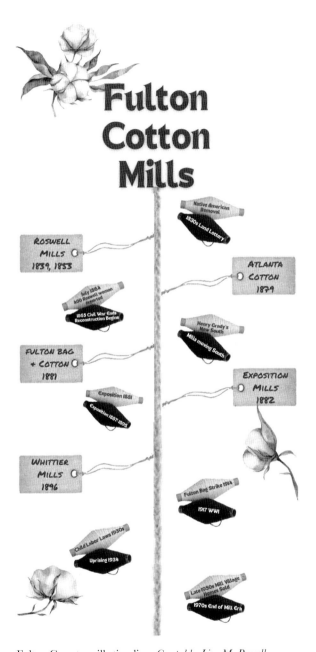

Fulton County mills timeline. *Created by Lisa M. Russell.*

My three sons know I do not suffer lazy. My middle son, Mike, is most like my father. He works long hours as a skilled mechanic in a manufacturing plant. After hours, while at home, he still works. He built a sawmill and a building on his property to provide extra income for his family. Though he met my father only once as a toddler, he somehow inherited the legacy of labor. I know he will pass it along to his children—especially his son, Wheeler.

These stories in this book may seem foreign to you. But all these stories about our collective past weave the threads together, and they cover us. Patches of the past are stitched together into a beautiful mess. The threads are knotted and cluttered on one side of the unfinished quilt. But turn it over and glimpse at the other side. The fine point is to cherish history, even our messy past with disjointed pieces. In the end, it makes sense and keeps us warm.

PART I

COTTON

Chapter 1

COTTON

THE FABRIC OF OUR LIVES

Despite his ninety-nine years, Henry Wright's memory was unclouded and intense. The five-foot, dark-skinned man was born on a plantation near Buckhead, Georgia. He remembered his time on another plantation outside Decatur. He remembered the horn blowing at 3:00 a.m. to wake the workers going to the fields. He said:

> When the time came to pick the cotton, each slave was required to pick at least 200 lbs. of cotton per day. For this purpose, each was given a bag and a large basket. The bag was hung around the neck, and the basket was placed at the end of the row. At the close of the day, the overseer met all hands at the scales with the lamp, the slate, and the whip. If any slave failed to pick the required 200 lbs. he was soundly whipped by the overseer.

Henry continued, "They were able to escape this whipping by giving illness as an excuse. Another form of strategy adopted by the slaves was to dampen the cotton or conceal stones in the baskets, either of which would make the cotton weigh more."

Emmaline was a child slave, and she remembered the women had weaving and spinning to do after coming in from the fields. Emmeline says her mother had to card or comb out the cotton at night so her two older sisters could begin spinning the following day on a loom. The loom was almost as large as a small kitchen. Spinning wheels hummed until midnight, when a bell rang and work was to cease.[6]

Emma Hurley of Washington, Georgia, remembered that in 1937, while she was a slave in Washington-Wilkes, Georgia, women always had work to do. During the Depression, the New Deal writers of the Federal Writers' Project interviewed Emma. They recorded her thoughts: "Each one was given the task of spinning six broaches a week. On Saturday, a white lady reeled off the spinning, and if one of the women had failed in her task, she was severely beaten."[7]

Cotton is to blame. A tagline designed to promote cotton in the twentieth century strangely fits eighteenth- and nineteenth-century life for enslaved African Americans: "Cotton: The fabric of our lives." Cotton profits were only possible for southern planters with free labor.

Fugitive slave John Brown explained in his book *Slave Life in Georgia: A Narrative of the Life, Sufferings, and Escape of John Brown, a Fugitive Slave, Now in England,* "Cotton is the King of Slaver. So long as there is a good market for slave-grown cotton, so long will it pay slaveholders to produce it."[8] And pay it did.

Slave labor was still entrenched in America when the Constitutional Convention was held. The delegates met in Philadelphia in the summer of 1787 to figure representation. Slavery was deeply entrenched in American society. It was a confusing mess. Though some felt all men were created equal, making that a reality was slow to come. Georgia and South Carolina wanted enslaved residents to be counted among white; northern states did not wish southern states to have an unfair advantage. So, there was a compromise. Enslaved men would count as three-fifths of a person. It was also decided that the abolition of the slave trade would occur in twenty years. Starting in 1807, slave traders could not bring Africans into the country, but this did not abolish the slave trade.[9]

Several Georgia planters received new cotton seeds from Loyalists who had fled the American Revolution to the Bahamas. This unique cotton flourished along the coast and soon became a massive hit in England. Exports doubled and doubled again.

In some ways, the South was more progressive than the North in the 1850s. Northern manufacturers seemed more advanced than the agrarian South, but the power was in the workforce. Without cheap cotton, the northern textile mills would cease spinning.[10]

Cotton picking was labor-intensive. The fibers or lint were difficult to pick without cutting fingers. The cotton grew only three feet off the ground, so workers had to stoop for hours extracting it. A hot thirteen-hour day produced only a pound of cotton per picker. The work was terrible and required much slave labor to make it profitable.

An odd document called "Cheap Cotton by Free Labor" promoted slave labor and boasted of the growth of slave labor that kept profits at a premium. In 1860, Georgia had the highest slave population at 462,230. That is a ten-year increase from 381,682 in 1850.[11]

According to History.com:

> *The slave economy had been very good to American prosperity. By the start of the war, the South was producing 75 percent of the world's cotton and creating more millionaires per capita in the Mississippi River valley than anywhere in the nation. Enslaved workers represented Southern planters' most significant investment—and the bulk of their wealth.*[12]

While the plantation owners were getting rich, the slaves worked day and night. After the sweaty fieldwork, they spent the night preparing the cotton for spinning. When they were not picking their daily quota, they picked cotton by firelight. They had to remove the seed from the lint and fibers. This painstaking task took hours, but the cotton worked better by firelight and warmth. Before Eli Whitney created the cotton gin, enslaved people could only pick out ten pounds of cotton daily. The gin (cotton engine) could process one hundred pounds per day. But the gin was not available yet, and their day was not done.

The next step was spinning the cotton into thread. The rough homespun was formed on spindles, and weaving began. Slaves not only had to produce their own clothes, but they also had to weave out sheets of cloth for the master's use. On some plantations, overseers beat the weary women when fabric production was low. Morning into the evening, cotton was the fabric of their lives.

Chapter 2

CHEAP COTTON

Cotton is an ancient plant that was around for thousands of years before it made its way into Georgia's history. In some cultures, it is a symbol of wealth and well-being, and it makes a perfect second-anniversary gift. Georgia planters bought and sold this staple and got rich on the backs of others—cheap cotton with free labor—but the cost was high. Slaves, sharecroppers, and millworkers paid the price much later.

Georgia was the first colony to produce cotton commercially. Europeans first grew cotton in coastal Georgia in 1734. Sea-island cotton was the first type grown in Georgia, but it could not be raised outside the coastal area. Following Native American removal in the 1830s, some land opened in other parts of the state. It was discovered that they could grow short-staple cotton in places other than the coast. Upland cotton did not need the coastal environment and proliferated with shorter fibers.

Tobacco farmers entering the Piedmont were eager to move into cotton; they just needed a better way to separate the lint from the seed. Enter Eli Whitney, the tinkerer who received a cotton engine patent in 1794. This invention changed the world of cotton production. Wait. Was it really Eli—or maybe someone else?

Two years before this, Catherine Greene hired Eli as her maintenance worker for her Savannah plantation. She was the wife of legendary Revolutionary War general Nathanael Greene. After General Greene died of sunstroke in 1786, he left her destitute to raise her five children alone on a cotton plantation. Catherine knew the cotton business. She taught Whitney about the struggle of separating the seed from the lint.[13]

The cotton gin Whitney first designed had wooden teeth and was a failure. He almost quit, but Catherine encouraged him to try again with wires; maybe her wire hairbrush inspired her. Whitney tinkered until he refined the old design. His (and Catherine's) invention used wires to grab and pull the lint from cotton seed and fed the cotton into a slatted box. Another roller with small brushes yanked the separated lint from the first roller. This simple idea would change cotton production forever. The financial repercussions were enormous for planters—and Whitney. Women could not apply for patents until near the turn of the twentieth century, so Whitney, not Catherine Greene, got the credit and the cash that came with this remarkable invention.

Every planter benefited, but Whitney overreached a little. Farmers were buying up this simple box. Initially, Whitney went all over Georgia installing gins. He required farmers to come to him and pay a fee. He charged two-fifths of the profit paid in cotton. The farmers rebelled and made their own versions of the gin. Catherine Greene and her new husband, Phineas Miller, financed Whitney and the legal battle that would ensue for years until the original patent expired. Whitney got all the credit but did not profit in the end.[14]

While Whitney (and Catherine) never got rich from the cotton gin, Georgia did. Raw cotton production doubled each decade after 1800. As spinning and weaving machines powered the Industrial Revolution, cotton demand soared. By 1850, America was growing three-quarters of the world's cotton.

Once harvested, cotton was easy to store and transport. Even small farmers grew it on every inch of their land, but big farmers with lots of slave labor were raking in the profits.[15] The cotton gin cut out some of the labor-intensive work. Manual labor could clean one pound of cotton daily, but the new gin could produce one hundred pounds. Slave labor could now focus on growing and picking, while the planters grew richer with free labor. Even though the slave trade from Africa ended in 1808, by 1860, Georgia had become the most prominent state using slaves.[16]

Instead of reducing the need for slaves, the use of the cotton gin increased this need. As production increased, they shipped more raw cotton to Great Britain and New England. Between 1801 and 1835, U.S. cotton exports grew from 100,000 bales to more than 1 million. Half of all U.S. exports were cotton. Cotton drove the southern economy, and slavery caused huge profits.[17] Cotton gave southerners the courage to go along with secession efforts.

They shipped most of the raw cotton north for textile production. Georgia had few cotton mills before the Civil War. Trion, Georgia, had an early mill in Northeast Georgia beginning in 1847. Trion Mills, now called Mount Vernon Mills, is still in production. In Douglas County, a mill community called Sweetwater opened Manchester Mills. This five-story factory opened in 1849. However, the earliest cotton mill in Georgia was in Cobb County, where Roswell King opened the Roswell Manufacturing Company in 1839. When the Civil War came to town, Roswell's mills were in full production. The mills were spinning and weaving until July 5, 1864, when Union general Kenner Garrard discovered the "Roswell Gray" coming off the looms. Sherman ordered him to cease the treasonous work of supplying Confederate uniform wool."

———◇✦◇———

FROM THE GROUND UP: COTTON IN THE FIELD

Upland cotton is the most common type of cotton grown in Georgia. It requires long growing seasons with lots of sunshine and slight frost.

Farmers plant Georgia cotton beginning in April and into early June. When everything is correct, seeds sprout and push through in two weeks. The young seedlings' first two visible leaves or cotyledons absorb sunlight into the plants. The leaves convert sunlight into carbohydrates. This is photosynthesis at work.

A week later, the first natural leaf grows and takes over the photosynthesis process from the first leaves. The plant grows when, five weeks later, a small flower bud forms. Another name for the bud is "squares." The squares swell, and buds inside push through the fringed leafy part, called bracts. By nine weeks, the white flowers bloom through photosynthesis. These flowers contain both male and female reproductive details that enable self-pollination.

These flowers do not mess around; pollination happens in hours, and by the second day, the flowers have a pink blush that changes to red by the third day. The flowers dry up and fall away in five to seven days, and a baby cotton boll appears.

These fruits (because each pod has seeds) grow thick fibers as the bolls grow, and then sixteen weeks after planting, the bolls split, revealing cotton. The dried burs or carpels (the segments) hold the locks of cotton and seeds. Three weeks later, the fiber has dried and fluffed and is ready for picking. Then it is off to the cotton gin.

. . . .

COTTON AND KUDZU

Cotton was an important crop and profitable even for small farmers. Every inch, up to the farmer's door, was planted year after year with cotton. This level of farming depletes the soil or nutrients and adds to the topsoil's erosion.

Pictures from the 1930s show treeless grand canyons of red dirt on Georgia farms. It looks like a foreign land compared to the lush green we now see in Georgia. Poor farming practices damaged the land. Erosion was severe, and a federal law established the Soil Conservation Service to address the problem. They started programs to teach farmers how to plant and plow. Farmers were trained to rotate crops. Still, erosion existed. So the Soil Conservation Service and local districts imported a solution and gave farmers certificates for planting a new miracle plant: kudzu.

We now know that kudzu was more of a curse than a miracle, but it did stop widespread erosion. Today, kudzu remains, but it eliminated the gulleys in farmland.[18]

. . . .

Erosion in North Georgia in 1938. This shows the damage to the land from over planting crops like cotton. *Courtesy of the National Archives.*

BOLL WEEVIL COMES TO TOWN

In 1915, a small beetle that feeds on cotton buds and flowers immigrated to Georgia from southern Mexico. The boll weevil infects the seeds and fibers and moves quickly to destroy entire crops.

According to the New Georgia Encyclopedia, "Yield losses associated with the boll weevil reduced cotton acreage from a historical high of 5.2 million acres during 1914 to 2.6 million acres in 1923."[19]

When pesticides did not work, the government instituted the Boll Weevil Eradication Program (BWEP). It was a trapping program that would destroy the entire crop when they found boll weevil in a field. Eventually, the little pest was eliminated. By the early 1990s, you did not see boll weevils in Georgia.

Today, we do not see boll weevils, but the eradication program is still in effect. A bright yellow trap is required in every cotton field. Private citizens who are not farmers may not grow cotton in the family garden. All cotton growers in Georgia are required to participate in the BWEP. The cotton growers funded these efforts.[20]

FROM FIELD TO FABRIC

Industrial technology has come a long way since the antebellum South and even the Industrial Revolution, but the essence of yarn production and fabric creation remains the same.
1. Workers open cotton bales weighing over five hundred pounds and mix different bales to blend fiber properties.
2. Next, to the carding rooms. Carding is separating and aligning the fibers.
3. The fibers are drawn through a funnel-shaped device called a trumpet, allowing a soft rope called a sliver (sounds like *driver*).
4. Eight strands of sliver are drawn into a roving frame that pulls or drafts the sliver out and gently twists. This is the first step of spinning yarn.

5. Spinning machines draw the roving and add a twist, making it tighter and thinner until it reaches the yarn thickness (or count) needed for weaving or knitting fabric. (Modern equipment eliminates the need for roving, and air jet and vortex use compressed air to stabilize yarn, removing the need for mechanical twisting.)

6. After spinning, machines tightly wind yarn around bobbins (tubes), and it is ready for fabric creation.

. . . .

WEAVING

Weaving is the oldest method for making yarn into fabric. Modern techniques are faster, but the basic principle of interlacing yarns remains the same. On a loom, lengthwise yarns called the warp form the skeleton of the fabric. The warp requires a higher twist than the filling yards that interlace width-wise.

In the old days, wooden huddles moved horizontally back and forth across the loom, interlacing the filling yard with the horizontal warp yard. Modern methods eliminate the shuttle, work at incredible speeds, and are much quieter.

Three basic weaves:

1. Plain weave: The filling is alternately passed over one warp yarn and under the next for gingham, percale, chambray, artistes, and other fabrics.

2. Twill weave: Yarns are interlaced to form diagonal ridges across the fabrics. This is used for tough fabrics: denim, gabardine, herringbone and ticking.

3. Satin weave: This is the least common and produces a smooth fabric with a high sheen. It is used for cotton sateen and made with fewer yarns interlacing and with either the warp or filling yarns dominating the "face" of the cloth.

. . . .

KNITTED FABRICS

Knitting is a method of constructing fabric using a series of needles to interlock loops of yarn. Lengthwise rows of these loops are called wales, comparable to the warp yarn in woven goods. Crosswise rows, similar to filling yarns, are called courses.

Cotton is knit on a circular machine with needles on the rim of a rotating cylinder. As the cylinder turns, needles do their work producing a fabric tube.

. . . .

Fabrics

Fabrics come from the loom in rough, unfinished materials and are called greige goods (pronounced *gray* goods). They require various finishing processes. Some mills dye or print and then finish. Others sell greige goods to converters that have cloth finished in other mills.

. . . .

Dyeing

The most common way to dye is piece and yarn dyeing. Piece dyeing is for a solid length of fabric pulled through the dye in a continuous hot dye solution. Then the material gets squeezed through a padded roll to remove excess and make the color even.

Another way is yarn dyeing before it is woven or knitted to create special effects. Blue-dyed warp yarns are combined with white-colored filling yarn to make blue jean material.

. . . .

Printing

Like printing on paper, long runs of the same fabric design with as many as ten different colors can be printed on one continuous roll.

A design is etched into rollers, and with tremendous pressure, the color is pressed into etching. The printed cloth is dried immediately.

. . . .

FINISHING

The final step in fabric production is finishing. Hundreds of finishes are applied with many methods of application. There are many ways to finish cotton to make it feel like cotton. Some finishes add a wrinkle-free element. There are durable press finishes. Other finishes are to make fabric water repellent or flame resistant or for shrinkage control.[21]

PART II

ROSWELL MANUFACTURING COMPANY

Chapter 3

REMNANTS

He staggered into town, ragged and torn from war. He had left Roswell, Georgia, early in the conflict with lofty ideals knit to his soul, but this Rebel returned unraveled. Before the war, mill owners had given him a home when he worked in Roswell mills, so he walked home. But another family was living there now. There was no trace of his wife and child, and no one had answers for him. They were missing along with hundreds of other women and children—gone girls, gone factory girls with children, and a few men.

He continued his walk through town. He inspected the remains of the three mills that once produced materials for the Confederates. This former Confederate soldier found broken threads of his life and pieces of his past. He looked for the six-hundred-foot covered bridge that crossed where Vickery Creek emptied into the Chattahoochee River. It was gone too. Fragments of fire accelerant were scattered where the bridge once crossed Vickery Creek. Pieces of cotton and wool scraps caused the wooden bridge to burn brilliantly on July 5, 1864. It would be years before he would know the story. For now, what spread out before him was a gaping hole where the bridge once stood. He knew he might never see his family again. He wondered, "And for what?"

History has left the events of July 1864 in tatters, while historians stitched together military records, a few letters and diaries from Federal soldiers. Piecemeal stories appeared in Northern newspapers, but they lost interest in August as the war continued to move south.

The victims of this war crime could not speak for themselves. They did not leave diaries or letters because most of these women were illiterate. General Garrard ordered them to bring only what they could carry, and they certainly left writing utensils behind. In addition, they had to survive every day on the train; when they disembarked in strange lands, they had to put one foot in front of another to provide for their families.

When primary sources are missing and we leave stories untold, fiction writers and story spinners rush in to fill the gaps, leaving the truth in pieces. History then weaves a fragile fabric of facts or what we call today "fake news." When we seek the actual story, all that remains are threads hanging from loose tapestries. We crave authenticity but must settle for inferior reproductions. Instead of history transforming our future, we are stuck with loose stitching and fragments of the past that leave us confused.

While the cotton mills of Sweetwater in Douglas County had more firsthand accounts and records, they left us little of the Roswell story. When we see through a glass dimly, sometimes the paranormal experts come in to bring in an additional dimension. Some of the best paranormal investigations are the ghost tours in Roswell. These experts infuse their walks with local history. The facts are correct, but introducing the supernatural is not using a primary source. So once again, we rely on legend and lore among broken tombstones.

In my last book, *Lost Mill Towns of North Georgia*, I included Roswell mills because the town was part of Cobb County at one time. I include them again in this book because Roswell is now in Fulton County; it was annexed in 1932. In my attempt to tell a curious story while honoring the truth, this was my opening to the Roswell chapter:

> *On July 5, 1864, a bell tolled in Roswell, Georgia, just before sunrise. The worker's alarm clock. Adeline Buice lies in her bed, pregnant with her fourth child, thinking about her husband. The Union army took him prisoner in 1863. She was not sure he would make it home. She forced herself up, prepared a last meager breakfast for her three children, and left them in the care of another. She did not know what this day would bring; and how nothing would ever be the same again.* [22]

Another scene continues with Buice introducing us to another factory girl. More fragmented facts are available:

> *Adeline noticed the unusual quiet as she walked toward the mill to start her shift. So many of the supervisors were gone, leaving the community empty.*

She went to the machine and began another long, hot day at Roswell Mills. She was not the only one lost in daydreams.

Georgiana Morgan, a young widow and mother of two, was on her job at the Woolen Mill at Roswell. As she made "Roswell Gray," the material used to sew into Confederate uniforms, Georgiana was thinking about her husband. She wondered if he was wearing the same gray wool for his uniform when he was buried in Mississippi the year before. Her thoughts were rudely interrupted as men with a Northern twang shouted orders.

"Get up and go home. Gather up everything you can carry, including your children, and come back here in two hours. You are all under arrest for treason by the authority of General William Tecumseh Sherman of the Army of the Potomac." Brigadier General Kenner Garrard's cavalry began its twelve-day occupation of Roswell. It began preparing the "prisoners for travel to the Marietta Square."[23]

Let's go back to the beginning of the Roswell colony when Roswell King sought gold in the hills near Auraria and stumbled on a well-watered area that piqued his interest. Let's get to know this man who named the town after himself.

Chapter 4

ROSWELL KING

B orn in 1765 in Windsor, Connecticut, Roswell King was an ambitious and entrepreneurial man. When he was twenty-three, he moved south to the Georgia coast. In 1788, he married Catherine Barrington, whose ancestry was part of the royal Tudors. She also had family ties to General James Oglethorpe, founder of the colony of Georgia. Roswell and Catherine had ten children, with five boys and two girls surviving adulthood.

Roswell had various careers and endeavors while living in Darien, Georgia. He was a well-respected builder known for his skill with a regional building material made of lime, shells, and sand called tabby. Stores, warehouses, and a large hotel were all built by him. He earned a position as the county surveyor and justice for the inferior court. King was a representative for the Georgia House in 1794. Before taking his most controversial work, he had a lifetime of experience.

In 1802, he became a plantation overseer for Philadelphia owner Major Pierce Butler on his Butler and St. Simons Island. This was a lucrative position with latitude. Major Butler did not want to live on the sultry coastal Georgia island, so he trusted King with the day-to-day management. He would oversee hundreds of Black slaves, and he was determined to keep this free labor healthy and working in the fields. King cared for this valuable commodity by feeding and clothing them, but he also demanded strict obedience. He did what was necessary to protect the investment. Butler's biographer, Malcolm Bell Jr., said Major Butler disagreed with the severity and frequency of King's beatings.[24]

Besides vicious whippings, King would split families for punishment or banish them. *The Women Will Howl* recorded, "The worst offenders were whipped and then banished to a horrible swamp in a remote corner of St. Simons Island, a penal colony called Five Pound Tree."[25]

King's reputation spread to other plantations, but he isolated his slaves. They could not attend church services like other slaves in the area. Other owners felt religion and church made for contented slaves, but not Roswell King. He felt they were spending too much time on religion, so he had an alternate plan. He asked Butler for funding to purchase a dozen fiddles to replace church and preaching with dancing. He thought they would sleep better if they danced instead of listening to preaching.

After eighteen years, Butler and King parted ways. This was not primarily due to King's abuse of Butler's slaves but to losing his valuable assets during the British invasion (1815). The British army convinced 138 slaves to board ships and leave for Britain instead of remaining on the Butler Plantation with Roswell King as the boss.

Recorded in *Butler's Legacy*, a biography by Bell, King wrote to Major Butler about the incident:

> *Negroes have neither honr or Gratitude. God cursed the Negroe by making him Black. I Curse the Man that brot the first from Africa, and the Curse of God is still on them, to send them away to die a miserble death....To treat Negroes with humanity is like giving Pearls to Swin, it is throwing away Value and giting insult and ingratitude in return.*[26]

Roswell did not understand why the slaves wanted to leave. He was bitter. Butler was angry at the loss of his valuable assets. Butler resigned in 1821 and left his son Roswell King Jr. to oversee the Butler plantations, but under the younger, the treatment of the slaves grew worse.

When Roswell returned to Darien, he was a wealthy man. He could choose his subsequent pursuit. At sixty-three years old, Roswell King mounted up and rode from Savannah to Auraria and Dahlonega for his new employer, the Darien Bank. In the 1830s, the North Georgia gold rush was on, and King wanted to be part of it, so he headed north. While working for the bank in 1833, he stayed in Auraria for several months. King was the cashier and on the board of directors of the branch. Roswell King left Auraria for that place that was calling him home.

In 1834 or 1835, Roswell returned to the land he had spotted two years before on his initial north visit to the gold grounds. He crossed the

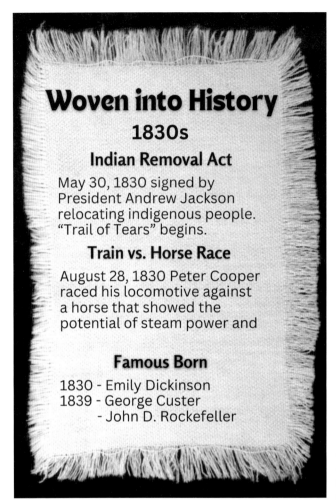

Woven into History

1830s

Indian Removal Act

May 30, 1830 signed by President Andrew Jackson relocating indigenous people. "Trail of Tears" begins.

Train vs. Horse Race

August 28, 1830 Peter Cooper raced his locomotive against a horse that showed the potential of steam power and

Famous Born

1830 - Emily Dickinson
1839 - George Custer
        - John D. Rockefeller

Created by Lisa M. Russell. Photo 15016031 by Valery Kraynov, Dreamstime.com.

Chattahoochee River and climbed a hill along Vickery Creek, named for a Native American woman who had lived nearby. While Cherokees lived around the creek and the Chattahoochee, the unspoiled hills, virgin hardwood, and pine drew King in. Darien's salty, swampy atmosphere starkly contrasted with North Georgia's crisp air. The coursing, clear river water added to the mystery of this enchanted land. Picture Roswell King on horseback surveying from the top of the hill, the land below as a perfect sanctuary for a new home and a final chapter of his life. Builder and entrepreneur King was going to build his kingdom; he would be one of the first to create a cotton mill in Georgia. He had found the perfect location to plant a town and build a water-powered mill.

Roswell King moved into this wilderness with a few neighbors, including some Cherokee farmers. He bought many of the forty-acre gold lots from men who had purchased them in the Georgia Land Lottery in 1832 and 1833. He offered investment opportunities to his friends and families living on the Georgia coast, along with stock options for a new cotton mill.

Along with his family and the few slaves he brought, King cleared the land and began building a log cabin for his family. The cabin expanded many times to accommodate the new arrivals. The family names of those who took King up on his investment were elite. Some names are part of Georgia's history and geography.

Roswell laid out the town like a New England colony, with wide streets radiating from the town square. The new families had to build homes. One person never to see the town was Catherine King. Roswell's wife died in 1839 before coming to the colony and is buried in Darien. She would never attend the Presbyterian church or be buried alongside her husband in the town founder's graveyard.

The town built the first proper home for Roswell's widowed daughter. Eliza lived with her children in Primrose Cottage, a New England–style two-story house, next to her brother Barrington. Later, Roswell moved in with his daughter and lived there until his death. Across the street was the first church.

The Roswell Presbyterian Church initially met in the Primrose Cottage until they built their church building. The church has existed since 1840. Roswell King's son-in-law was the first pastor.

Barrington King chose a home spot above all the others with a view of the village. From his roof, he could walk around to see the mill, Vickery Creek, and the Chattahoochee River. This home still survives, and some say Margaret Mitchell patterned Tara partly after Barrington Hall.[27] The Hall and its landscaping invite couples (including my son and his fiancée) to come for beautiful wedding and engagement photos.

Major James Stephens Bulloch was an old family friend of Roswell King. They persuaded him to move from Savannah to the new Roswell colony. He lived in the log cabin with the Kings until he built Bulloch Hall. It is standing today, with its claim to fame as the home and wedding venue of President Theodore Roosevelt's parents, on December 22, 1853. TR visited Roswell often. Six families founded Roswell around the same time.

The founding families replaced King's original communal log home that began the wilderness colony. Still standing are Barrington Hall, Bulloch Hall, Primrose Cottage, Great Oaks, Mimosa Hall, and the Smith Plantation.

Roswell Mill's source of power. A human-made water falls on Vickery Creek still flows. *Author's collection.*

The original rock wall of Roswell Manufacturing Company. *Author's collection.*

The Roswell Chapter of the United Daughters of the Confederacy placed a marker in the town square in 1940 to honor the six founding members. King also was honored with a plaque at his town square in 1939.

One group that failed to be recognized for their contribution was the factory workers who provided inexpensive labor for these founding members. It was not until 2000 that the Roswell Mills Camp #1547, Sons of Confederate Veterans, placed a ten-foot-tall granite Corinthian column. This memorial to the Roswell women guaranteed millworkers would never be forgotten.[28]

With the town situated, Roswell King began building the Roswell Manufacturing Company. The cotton mill was ready to spin in 1839. His son Barrington became president after Roswell's death on February 15, 1844.

Barrington built a second mill in 1850. The Ivy Woolen Mill rose with two of Barrington's sons in charge. The woolen mills created a well-made cloth called Roswell Gray.[29]

Chapter 5

JULY 1864

He had his orders. He had to compensate for his last disappointment because his boss could be moody and punitive. Roswell was his chance to redeem his career. Though it was not the finest hour for the Union army, Garrard followed orders in Roswell after he failed at Resaca.

Brigadier General Kenner Garrard led the Second U.S. Cavalry in the Atlanta Campaign when he was thirty-seven. The West Point graduate had bouts of self-doubt, or maybe he was being overly cautious. His indecision was not a good look for this well-equipped division. When General Sherman ordered Garrard to destroy railroad tracks at Resaca, he worried and joined the rest of the army. His boss was not pleased. Sherman wrote, "I regret exceedingly you did not avail yourself of the chance I gave you to cut the railroad. I want you to dash in and strike the retreating masses in the flank and all around. Do not spare horseflesh but strike boldly."[30]

On July 5, 1864, General Garrard's soldiers were fighting the Roswell Guard. The bridge over the Chattahoochee was crucial for troop transport to the Atlanta Campaign, so the Roswell battalion burned it on their way out of town. While it burned, the factories spun away, and the workers stayed.

When Garrard inspected the scene, he noticed a flag that had not been there when he sketched the factory town days before. Flying above the Ivy Woolen Mill was a French flag. Going through the mill, Garrard noticed the gray wool had the initials "CSA" woven into the cloth. He arrested the mill manager, French national Theophile Roche; he claimed partial ownership and thought flying his French banner would save the mill. Garrard discovered records showing the enemy used the Roswell Gray. Roche's ruse did not work, as he was arrested with the factory workers.

Besides the Ivy Woolen Mill producing uniform wool, the Roswell Manufacturing Company supplied the Confederates with sheeting, tenting, yarn, and rope. On July 6, 1864, as General Garrard looked on, the factories were in full production.

Union private Silas C. Stevens of the Chicago Board of Trade Battery described what happened next in a letter home:

> *The women and children filed out of the structure at once in quiet wonder on the banks of the stream, watching our preparations for the destruction of the mills. It did seem, at first blush, to be a wanton act, to fire these polished machines, which filled the building from the basement to the top story after they came to a standstill. But all is fair, as has been stated, in love and war.*

Garrard ordered the Ivy Woolen Mill burned. Then, moving upstream to the larger Roswell manufacturing mill, he set it ablaze. Before the fires, Yankee soldiers arrested four hundred workers, including eighty-seven Confederate deserters and older millworkers; the rest were women and children. They marched or carried these prisoners of war in wagons, accused of treason for producing materials for the enemy. They met with Sweetwater Creek factory girls from Douglas County to Marietta. Then they were imprisoned in the abandoned Georgia Military Institute. Some locals paid a fee to have some women stay in Marietta to work instead of shipping them north. Some women were raped and mistreated while waiting for transport.

Around July 15, 1864, they left Marietta, where the soldiers herded them into suffocating, hot trains. Like cattle, the women, young children, and a few men unfit for military service were shipped off. The women were given only nine days of rations. They could not leave notes, and most could not write or keep journals on their forced evacuation. Where they were going they did not know, but it was north.

These facts are supported by Sherman's own words to Garrard:

> *I repeat my orders that you arrest all people, male and female, connected with those factories, no matter what the clamor, and let them foot it, under guard, to Marietta, whence I will send them by cars to the North.…The poor women will make a howl. Let them take along their children and clothing, providing they have the means of hauling, or you can spare them.*[31]

A soldier described to his mother this event:

Dear Mother,
Received your kind letter yesterday and was glad to hear from you and to
hear that you was all well and I hope these few lines will find you all
the same and your letter found me in the best of health mother since i rote
before we have gin on forse march of 16 miles it was awful warm and
there was lots of the boys fel out and a good many were sunstroke and
some died out of the brigade or division that was on the march we went
up the river to Roswell there was a nise little town there and we burnt
two cotton factories and one woolen factorie and all the public buildings
in that plase and the fun was we had a chanse to see som of the georgia
wimen there was a bout 400 hundred factories girls and we had a fine
time with them there was some of them was very good looking we are
within about 8 miles of Atlanta.

Edwen C. Woodworth[32]

Weeks before these July events, Brigadier General Kenner Garrard sketched a map of Roswell. He was waiting and planning his attack in the Second Cavalry Division and the Third Brigade camp. On his map, he wrote in the margins, "Roswell is a very pretty factory town of about four thousand inhabitants. Mills and private property are not injured by me."

After the invasion and burning, he prepared his reports for delivery to Sherman. Before giving it to the courier at the last minute, he revised his sketched map. He edited his marginalia: "Roswell is a very pretty factory town of about four thousand inhabitants. ~~Mills~~ and private property are not injured by me."[33]

He crossed out the word *mills*.

On July 10, 1864, the trains began a journey taking the "prisoners with only the possessions they could carry." They made their way through North Georgia, stopped in Kingston, and then their train traveled through the Adairsville Depot. Next was Dalton and Tunnel Hill and then north to Chattanooga, Tennessee, for a short layover.

The first of many destinations was Nashville, where some women and children were left behind. The next stop was Louisville, Kentucky. This was the final destination for many of the millworkers. On July 21, the *Louisville Daily Journal* reported, "The train which arrived from Nashville last evening brought up 249 women and children from the south, who are sent here by

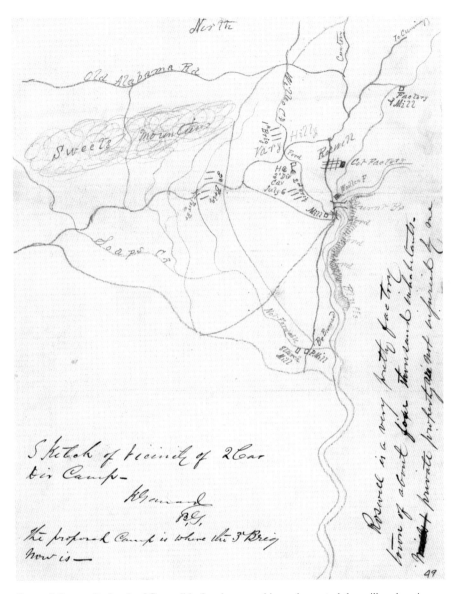

General Garrard's sketch of Roswell before he moved in and arrested the millworkers in July 1864. *Library of Congress.*

order of General Sherman….Why they should be sent here to be transferred North is more than we can understand."

Some prisoners were initially left in a Union hospital, where the medical staff treated the prisoners who were ill with fevers and various diseases. They

The Roswell women would have stopped at or traveled past the Adairsville Depot on their way north as traitors to the Union. This is the original depot in the early 1900s. *Courtesy of Adairsville History Museum.*

forced those released to take an oath of allegiance to the Union. For a time, the Louisville refugee hospital housed the women and children. Eventually, they all left to find a place to work and live. A few remained in the Louisville women's prison until April 1865.

Many Roswell women were taken farther north across the Ohio River and into Indiana. They found millwork, but they struggled. Some worked in a new mill after the war, and others just resorted to prostitution to survive. Very few returned to Roswell.

These women could not tell us their stories. Most were illiterate. Eventually, many factory girls remarried, not knowing if their husbands were alive. Many men returned to Roswell, gave up on finding their families and moved on with new wives and families.[34]

Back in Georgia, the war continued to a devastating end. Garrard's men moved on with the Atlanta Campaign, went east and found success in the Covington raid. Sherman continued to the sea, leaving a demoralized citizenry. On September 2, 1864, the Union army captured Atlanta and moved on in two different directions. The state capital in Milledgeville quietly surrendered in November. The path to Savannah left scorched towns and ransacked homes. Sherman left the people hungry and desperate.

On December 22, 1864, General Sherman sent a telegram and offered President Abraham Lincoln a Christmas present. He had ended his March to the Sea and captured Savannah. Sherman offered Lincoln the city along with 150 heavy guns, ammunition, and twenty-five thousand bales of cotton. According to the National Archives, "President Lincoln was thrilled to hear this news, which he immediately publicized throughout the nation."[35]

The Roswell incident might have been just another day for Sherman, but it changed hundreds of lives when his orders destroyed the mills.[36] After the war, General William T. Sherman was reprimanded by the U.S. government for issuing calloused and degrading orders against these poor, defenseless mill women. Sherman never mentioned the arrest and deportation of these four hundred women and children in his memoirs. Some historians say he never told his wife of these shameful events.

Before the war moved on, and only for a fleeting time, Northern and Southern newspapers condemned Sherman's actions against the Roswell women and children who were just working to survive. The *New York Tribune* reported, "Only think of it! Four hundred weeping and terrified Ellens, Susans and Maggies transported, in the springless and seatless army wagons, away from their lovers, and brothers of the sunny south, and all for the offense of weaving tent cloth and spinning stocking yarn."

The article disturbed General Grenville M. Dodge, commander of Sherman's XVI Corps. He opened his wallet, gave his chief surgeon $100 and ordered him to hire some Roswell girls. The *Patriot and Union*, a Pennsylvania newspaper, condemned Sherman:

> *It is hardly conceivable that an officer bearing a United States commission of Major General should have so far forgotten the commonest dictates of decency and humanity…as to drive four hundred penniless girls hundreds of miles away from their homes and friends to seek livelihood amid strange and hostile people. We repeat our earnest hope that further information may redeem the name of General Sherman and our own from this frightful disgrace.*

The King family and other mill owners left town early to escape Union occupation. They knew ahead of time, so they left behind their homes, the mills, and the workers. The Roswell elite thought more of the factory machinery and the remaining product they banked before leaving town. They gave little thought to the workers who kept working in their mills.

For the women and children traveling north under guard, their future was uncertain as the North Georgia mountains faded into the distance. What was certain was that there was little chance they would ever see Georgia again. Sherman's only concern was that they no longer supplied cloth to the enemy. He did not care what they did after he dropped them north. For a time, history forgot them as well.

ADELINE BAGLEY VENABLE BUICE

Adeline was thirty-nine years old and working in Roswell Manufacturing Mills when Yankee soldiers arrested her with four hundred other women and children. Her crime, according to Generals Sherman and Garrard, was treason. They lined up the workers and forced them to gather what they could carry and report to the army wagons for a fifteen-mile bumpy ride to Marietta. After several hours—three or four, most likely—Adeline Bagley Venable Buice ended up at the Georgia Military Institute with children in tow and one inside.

We learn a lot about Adeline Buice from her grave markers, both her original one and the one replaced by the Sons of the Confederacy. Between her birthdate in 1825 and her death in 1910, there is a simple hyphen that was an entire life. The stone focuses on only a few things and one portion of her life:

> Roswell Mill Worker Caught and Exiled to Chicago by Yankee Army 1864—Returned on Foot 1869

A blog by Traci Rylands and the Find a Grave website answer more questions. Adeline is buried in Cumming, Georgia, at the Sharon Baptist Church Cemetery, sometimes called the Sharon Cemetery. A broken and worn 1910 gravestone rests behind the new stone placed by a local chapter of the Sons of the Confederacy.

According to Find a Grave, Adeline had two husbands and six children. She had at least two children with her first husband, Sanford Venable. Richard Venable was fifteen and Evaline Venable was twelve when they were arrested for working in the mills with their pregnant mother in July

1864. Two other children, William M. Buice and Salena (Buice) Thompson, would have been younger than the Venable children. Still, there is no listing of their ages or what happened to them. We know Joshua had a daughter born while he was a refugee up north in 1864.

Joshua and Adeline were separated, but they found each other again at some point. Six children were born. Joshua and Adeline shared a son, John Henry Buice, born in 1867. This means either Joshua found his family in Chicago and they returned to Georgia together, or there is another explanation. Maybe Adeline returned five years later in 1869 with a two-year-old son, and Joshua stepped up. Some accounts suggest Joshua thought they were all dead, and he remarried. This happened a lot in Roswell at the time—men remarried after finding their factory girls gone. Like everything else about these women of Roswell, there are more questions than answers.[37]

SYNTHIA CATHERINE STEWART BOYD

In 1947, Synthia Catherine Stewart Boyd's grandson used a reel-to-reel tape recorder to capture her story. With "remarkable recall," they preserved her arrest as a ten-year-old in what she called the "Factory Town." Boyd was ninety-two years old when she remembered the events of July 6, 1864.

Her father, Walter Stewart, was a mill boss at Roswell Manufacturing during the war. Still, he enlisted with his cousin in 1862. With no income, his wife, Charlotte, and her mother went to work in the mills. It is unclear if Synthia, a nine-year-old girl, was also working in the mill. She had an older sister and a younger brother.

She remembered the trauma of being loaded into a troop train in Marietta. Mill women, children, and elderly men were packed into these trains with no food, no money—only the clothes they wore.

In her own words, Synthia remembered:

> *The Northern soldiers came to Roswell and made everybody leave the factory. They set it afire, and all the women and children cried as they watched it burn. The soldiers told the women to go home and fetch only what they could carry in their arms. We spent that night sleeping on the ground by the burned-out river bridge. The next morning, they took us all in wagons to Marietta and put us in a big building. (Marietta Military Institute emptied when the students went to war.)*

They didn't feed us much of nothing, and then they put us on troop trains and hauled us to Nashville and then to Louisville, Ky., and put us in a big hospital building with a high fence all around it. They called us "prisoners." One day we heard a band playing and saw soldiers marching by and we knew it meant they had taken more Southern soldiers prisoners. Our Uncle James, who had rheumatism and couldn't go to war, was there with us and got permission to take us kids to watch the prisoners march by. And there, in the bunch that marched by us, right back of the band, we saw our own Pa. But he didn't see us.

Uncle James got a pass for him and mother to go to the barracks and see Pa before they sent the prisoners over the river to Camp Chase in Ohio. Pa had been taken prisoner near Atlanta a month after we were taken away from home. When Pa and Ma saw each other, they cried with joy. Each thought the other was dead.

Ma got a job working for the Northern government in a mill, and she found a house for us to live in. Pa nearly starved to death in prison, but he managed to live there 10 months until the war ended. Then he came and lived with us and found work in a tannery in Louisville. After a while we were able to move back to Georgia. We found our house there in fair shape, but nothing was left in it. Pa got work helping to rebuild the mills. Some mill women died, some remarried, others were able to save enough to return home. But most were not as fortunate as we were.[38]

The Memorial—Finally

After the initial attention given to the Roswell women in the newspapers in the summer of 1864, they forgot the plight of these four hundred for other war news. This is one Civil War story that was not written in the history books. A few historians in the 1980s told the story. In 1998, the Roswell Mills Camp #1547 of the Sons of Confederate Veterans began the project to honor these forgotten factory workers.

To find descendants, they reached out through advertising and marketing. Most of the deported millworkers had settled in the North. After raising funds, the Sons of Confederate Veterans placed a ten-foot Corinthian column in Old Mill Park surrounded by restored mill village homes. The column is shattered at the top as a metaphor memorializing over four hundred crumbled lives. The ceremony was held on July 8, 2000. This date

Roswell millworkers' monument. *Author's collection.*

is significant. On that day 136 years before, the Roswell women, children, and a few men were arrested for treason.[39]

In Michael Hitt's book *Charged with Treason: Ordeal of 400 Mill Workers During Military Operations in Roswell, Georgia, 1864–1865*, he lists the names of the millworkers arrested for treason and sent north. What we do not know is all their stories. Most refugees would not have had the tools to keep journals of their journey. Many could not write and leave their stories behind, even if they had tools for writing. The memorial is a sculpture of a crumbling column standing near the former mill and village as a memorial to their untold stories. The inscription reads, "The monument was made public in 2000, following a rise in interest in the tragedies that surrounded the deportation, which had been largely forgotten in the aftermath of the Civil War."

Chapter 6

THE RECONSTRUCTION
OF ROSWELL

Rumors of Roswell ran rampant in the summer of 1864. Since most of the monied families had escaped the horrors of July 1864 in Roswell, no one knew what had happened. The Roswell Battalion had moved out before the bridge burned, and the other men in Confederate uniforms scattered.

Barrington Simeral King, Barrington's fifth son, was stationed in Virginia when he heard rumors about his hometown, so he wrote to his mother. Most of the stories were wrong. They heard that the Yankees burned the mills and the village. They also heard that Garrard burned the woolen mill but left the cotton mills to produce for their benefit. And they heard they burned the factories under the British flag. Pieces of truth.[40]

Barrington King was worried about his house, Barrington Hall. He heard they had torched it. He was very concerned a month after the Roswell occupation. They had prepared for the factories' destruction by storing cotton in warehouses throughout the state. King was far more worried about his home. Federals and some locals ransacked Barrington Hall, but the soldiers did not destroy it. Most of the elite homes were in the same condition. The Federal soldiers burned only the mills.

The King family wrote many letters about the Roswell events in July 1864. Many of the wealthy, elite families wrote notes about the condition of the town. Not one of the surviving letters from July and August 1864 mentioned the four hundred women and children arrested for the crime of working their mills before they were burned. No one even wondered where they were or considered looking for them to bring them home. The elite families could have provided the means to get their workers home. Still, they made no mention of these people until September.

The letters written in September 1864 between the families began mentioning the factory women, but not out of concern for their safety. There were reports of the houses still standing, but someone had trashed them from "top to bottom." A letter from the Smith family seemed to blame the workers.

William Smith wrote to his mother on September 7, 1864. He relayed a message of family friends seeing the trains with the factory girls moving north. The Presbyterian minister Nathaniel Pratt reported the damage to the homes. Later, Anne Smith wrote back to her son William commenting on "those people" when she said, "It is nothing more than I expected of those people when they had things in their power."[41] Barrington King added to the narrative, "We have done so much for that class of people, but they have no gratitude and now shew what we had to manage."[42] This is evidence of the mill owner's bitter hatred for his workers.

When Barrington made plans to rebuild one of the mills in 1865, he made it clear that he would not hire any of the former employees even if they made it back home. The stockholders of the Roswell Manufacturing Company met in 1865 to detail the destruction of the mills. They reported minor damage to the store building and the mill village homes, and Barrington King blamed the operatives.

> We regret much to report the conduct of a few men in our employment for years with the women and children from whom we expected protection to our property. They plundered and destroyed to a large amount, tearing down the shelves in the store to burn, breaking glasses and otherwise injuring the houses, hauling off iron and copper to sell, and putting the wheel in motion and seriously injuring it by throwing down rocks.[43]

When could these workers have had time to do this destruction? The timeline did not fit. The Yankees arrested and rounded up all the workers and sent them to Marietta within hours of leaving the mills. They were under guard the entire time and would not have had the chance to pillage. According to Mary Deborah Petite in her book *The Women Will Howl*, "Quick to condemn the workers for real or imagined offenses, the Roswell elite showed little consideration for the exiled workers. Not one expression of concern or compassionate sentiment can be found in their letters. No one even seemed curious as to the fate of so many displaced women and children."[44]

The Roswell Manufacturing Company's stockholders rebuilt as soon as possible. The 1854 building had a solid foundation, machine shop, and cotton house. In 1867, the mill was running again. Barrington King would not be present at the mill reopening. A horse kicked him in the chest, and he died in January 1866. He was buried at the Presbyterian church. The King family lost control of Roswell Manufacturing Company when his estate was divided. Because of Reconstruction taxes, his widow, Catherine Nephew King, had to sell most of her stock in the company to Andrew Jackson Hansell.[45] According to a June 6, 1873 report in the *Marietta Journal and Courier*, with factory improvements, "they are now making over 30,000 yards of excellent standard sheeting and shirting weekly. President Hansell is the right man to manage this splendid piece of property."

Under new ownership, the mills were running, and in 1872 they added a new mill wheel even with the problematic reliance on water power. In 1877, a turbine replaced the original water wheel. Turbine blades sit vertically, and water from the raceway funneled up against the blade, forcing an axle to spin. Shafts, gears, belts, and pulleys ran through the building. Water was still an issue. During droughts and floods, the water flow caused slowdowns and days of lost productivity.

Even with the 1897 upgrade to a wood-fired steam generator, creek water was still needed. Eventually, in 1898, hydroelectricity was used to power the new 1882 mill. By 1911, they used power in the older 1853 mill and the entire mill operation. In 1928, Georgia Power connected electricity to the mill, thus ending dependence on water power.

Flood damaged one of the mills in 1881, and in 1882, the company built a new mill on the hill above the earlier mill complex. In the 1880s and 1890s, Roswell Cotton Mills was known for sheeting, shirting, and other finished products sent across the South and all points north.

DAM FLOODING

The New South grew, but by 1900, the need for electricity prompted Atlanta's leader to invest in hydroelectric power. In 1901, the Atlanta Water and Electric Power company began constructing a hydroelectric dam. The city's first water-generated electricity dam, completed in 1904, was built on a section of the Chattahoochee River that would positively and negatively affect the Roswell Manufacturing Company.

Roswell, Georgia, 1900. Laurel Mills and workers. *Courtesy of the Roswell Historical Society.*

The dammed Chattahoochee River formed the Bull Sluice Lake in Sandy Springs. Now part of the Chattahoochee River National Recreation Area, the Morgan Falls dam is 1,031 feet long and 56 feet high. Morgan Smith, the original investor, died before they completed the dam. The Atlanta Water and Electric Company named the dam for Smith. Morgan Falls Dam became part of the Georgia Power Company and is still used to power Atlanta today.[46]

After Federal troops burned Ivy Mills in 1864, the owners built another woolen mill beside it. In 1881, Laurel Mills bought Ivy Mills and incorporated it. When Morgan Falls Dam opened, Laurel Mills suffered ongoing flooding. The mills were abandoned, and in 1916, the machinery was sold because of water damage. Rumor has it that the mill's last wool product was Roswell Gray for the American troops in World War I.[47]

In 1919, Laurel Mills sued Georgia Power for $152,000 in water damage caused by Morgan Falls Dam. I found no record detailing the outcome of this case.

Another fire ended the life of Roswell Mills. The mill, sold for $800,000 in 1920 to a South Carolina mill, seemed cursed.[48]

In 1926, lightning struck. The mill floors were saturated with machine oil, and the cotton created a tinderbox. The old mill went up and caused $400,000 worth of damage.[49]

The 1930s were difficult with the Great Depression and FDR's New Deal rules that led to the Great Uprising Textile Strike in 1934. Mill owners closed Roswell to protect the buildings from the strikers and violence like in other mills in Georgia.

Southern Hills bought Roswell Mills in 1941 and updated the buildings. To survive, the mills made laundry netting and carpet backing. The mill produced its last bolt of cotton cloth in 1975. Foreign competition was infecting the entire textile industry in the county.

WHAT REMAINS TODAY

The entire area underwent rejuvenation and reconstruction of another covered bridge over Vickery Creek. Today, the site is part of Atlanta's Chattahoochee River National Recreation Area. A covered pedestrian bridge over the creek connects the walking trail from Old Mill Park to the Chattahoochee River trail system. The covered bridge leads to the Chattahoochee Nature Center.

Rising two stories in the woods above the creek, hidden behind the brush, are the remains of many iterations of Roswell Manufacturing Company— crumbling brick walls and metal ghosts of old water mill works that powered the old mills.

In 2008, the city hired contractors to uncover the remains and create a historic walkway along the creek to the falls. The rusty remains of the 1880s include the massive turbine that powered the mill and an extensive iron flume that carried water from a dam on Vickery Creek to the turbine. A beautifully restored 1854 machine shop, as it was in the nineteenth century, stands beside the bridge along the creek.[50]

In 1987, the Roswell Mills were spinning again, but in a different way. April and Craig Bloomer opened Events Catering and turned the old 1882 Roswell Mill building into a historic venue. With areas in the space called Ivy Hall and Vickery Room, the Roswell Mill comes alive at weddings and special events. The surrounding area is filled with the romance of history with a rebuilt covered bridge and boardwalks leading to mill ruins along Vickery (now called Big) Creek. The walk leads to the falls that once powered the mills.

Opposite, top: Roswell Manufacturing mechanic shop on the banks of Vickery Creek. This is all that remains of the original mill except the rock walls. Refurbished. *Photo taken in 2022 by author.*

Opposite, bottom: Southern Mills in Roswell, Georgia. The mill closed in 1975. They converted it to a shopping complex in 1985 and now serves as a venue. *Courtesy of Roswell Historical Society.*

Above: Southern Mills repurposed for an event venue, 2022. *Author's collection.*

In 2018, Phase III of the Old Mill Park Trail Extension expanded the trails near the mill and added boardwalks with overlooks, making the area accessible. The trail made the final connections with the restored covered bridge and historic mill. The elevated boardwalk allows visitors to see the turbine that powered the mill until its closing in 1975.[51]

Roswell Cotton Mills

1839   Roswell Manufacturing Company opens Mill #1.

1853   Mill #2 and the second dam open.

1864   Both mills are burned at the hands of General Garrard during his occupation of Roswell.

1866   The 1853 mill (Mill #2) is rebuilt after the Civil War; it is now Mill #1.

1882   Roswell Manufacturing Company builds another mill. The rebuilt 1853 mill is called Mill #1, and the 1882 mill is Mill #2.

1894   Oxbow Falls Manufacturing Company (the Roswell Company) opens a cotton mill. It is later called the Pants Factory.

1900   A covered bridge is rebuilt over Vickery Creek.

1920   The Roswell Manufacturing Company is purchased, and its name is changed to Roswell Mills.

1926   Lightning destroys the 1853 mill (Mill #1) on June 12, and it is not rebuilt. The 1882 mill (Mill #2) was expanded and operated until 1975. It is known simply as "The Mill."

1930	The Great Depression brings difficulties. The 1934 strikes cause the mill to shut down for a time—just like other mills in the South.
1941	The Pants Factory is destroyed by fire, but a new building is constructed in 1942 (cost: $75,047).
1947	Southern Mills purchased the Roswell Mills and operated until 1975.
1974	The mills are listed in the National Register of Historic Places.
1975	Southern Mills closes. The covered bridge is abandoned.
1980	A new company producing jeans occupies the mill and then goes bankrupt while payroll checks bounce.
1982	Mimms Enterprises purchases the 1882 mill to create retail space.
1991	April and Craig Bloomer buy the 1882 mill and bring it back to life as an event facility called the Roswell Mill Club.
2005	The Vickery Creek Covered Bridge is built and crosses Vickery Creek. It connects the Vickery Creek Unit of the Chattahoochee River National Recreation Area to Roswell Mill.
2008	Roswell hires contractors to uncover the remains and create a historic walkway along the creek.

Roswell Woolen Mill

1857	James R. King and Thomas E. King establish Ivy Mills. Ivy Mills is not part of Roswell Manufacturing Company.
1864	Ivy Mills is destroyed during the Civil War; another mill is built next to the Ivy Mill site after the war. This would later be called Laurel Mill.
1873	Laurel Mills Manufacturing Company is incorporated.
1877	Laurel Mills purchases Empire Mills.
1904	Morgan Falls Dam is completed by the Atlanta Power and Water Company. Following completion, Laurel Mills experiences ongoing flooding.
1916	Laurel Mills is abandoned, and machinery is sold because of flood damage.
1919	Laurel Mills files suit against Georgia Power for flood damage.

PART III

THE EXPOSITIONS

Chapter 7

THE NEW SOUTH EXPOSED

C otton was still king, though the Civil War left a mess in Georgia. Only a few mills in Georgia produced cloth before the Civil War. And the defeated ones rose again. By 1870, Roswell Manufacturing Company had shaken off destruction and rebuilt its mills.

In the meantime, a few new mills opened. For example, the Atlanta Cotton Factory, the first cotton mill in Fulton County, opened in 1879. Henry Grady was on a mission. He encouraged H.I. Kimball to open this cotton factory. Grady's drive to promote the South with his cotton-to-the-mill mantra would bring more economic growth to Georgia.

Cotton in the nineteenth century was like crude oil in our century. E. Culpepper Clark in *The Birth of a New South* wrote, "When compared with oil, the American South was to become Saudi Arabia for cotton.[52] In *Empire of Cotton*, Sven Beckert quoted John Greenleaf Whittier's poem calling cotton the "Haschish of the West."[53] So when the Civil War dried up the supply, there was worldwide withdrawal. Exports in 1860 were 3.8 million bales and dropped to almost nothing in 1862.[54] But cotton came back.

Atlanta Cotton Mills from the *Atlanta Guidebook. Historic Atlanta Guidebook Images, Southern Labor Archives. Special Collections and Archives, Georgia State University, Atlanta.*

H.I. Kimball, Atlanta business leader who started Atlanta Cotton Factory (Mill) in 1879 and was the executive director of the 1885 Cotton Exposition. His hotels were famous luxury destinations in Atlanta, including the Kimball House. *Historic Atlanta Guidebook Images, Southern Labor Archives. Special Collections and Archives, Georgia State University, Atlanta.*

The South returned to prewar cotton production by 1870. Sharecroppers, small family farmers, and planters had doubled output by 1891.[55] According to Clark, "A bale of a five-acre plot was worth as much as a bale" at a plantation.[56] Cotton remained king, and the South still produced and shipped it north. But the more profitable piece was missing. The real money was in manufacturing. Taking the cotton from the field to the mill would cut out the expense of exports. Enter Henry Grady.

HENRY GRADY

His name is on a hospital, a journalism school at the University of Georgia, and a statue in downtown Atlanta. A quick Google search exposes the shady side of this man. Grady is now controversial because of his unfortunate associations and subtle snubs. He has paid for it with the removal of his name from an Atlanta middle school. Also, a group of Georgia State students wanted to remove Grady's statue from downtown. But thanks to State Senate Bill 77, the monument was saved from removal and vandalism.[57]

A deeper internet dive uncovers that Henry Grady is due recognition. Condemn him for poor associations, but do not ignore what he did for Georgia. We need to remember what he did to bring industry to Georgia. He helped Atlanta out of the ashes to become a phoenix city. Ironically, the two women sitting at the base of his statue symbolize history and memory.

In my book *Lost Mill Towns of North Georgia*, I wrote about the day Grady went to New York on behalf of his beloved South:

> *North Georgia native and Southern journalist Henry W. Grady was invited to speak, but he didn't want to do it. The New England Society of New York City invited Grady to speak. They picked him because they read his columns that were informed, conservative, and industry friendly. On December 22, 1886 in a crowded Delmonico's restaurant Grady was on the roster to speak, but not until General William Tecumseh Sherman spoke. Just after he finished, the band played "Marching Through Georgia." The antagonist mood was set for Henry Grady to talk about "The New South."*
>
> *Grady began with a quote:*
> *"There was a South of slavery and succession—that South is dead. There is a South of Union and freedom—that South, thank God, is living breathing, growing every hour." Grady quotes Benjamin H. Hill at Tammany Hall in 1866 and goes on to describe the South in Reconstruction. He uses vivid images of the northern soldier and the southern soldier returning home. One comes home to plenty of work and home they remember and the other comes home to poverty and destroyed homes. Grady shares the attitude of most defeated southerners when he quoted Georgia author Bill Arp, "Well, I killed as many of them as they did of me and now I'm going to work."*
>
> *Grady said, "There is a new south, not through protest against the old, but because of new conditions, new adjustments and, if you please, new ideas and aspirations."*

He points out that the southern cotton crop brought in $400,000,000 annually and notes that if they produce textiles near the crop, they would get rich. He reminds them of dropped interest rates for industry from 24 to 6 percent. Grady tells the northern industrialists that the path is smooth and the Mason and Dixon line has been erased. He does mention the "negro problem," but ensures them this is under control (an overestimate on Grady's part). He concludes by recognizing the difficulties between the states and quotes this stanza:

"Those opposed eyes,
which like the meteors of a troubled heaven,
All of one nature, of one substance bred,
Did lately meeting in th' intestine shock,
Shall now, in mutual well beseeming ranks,
March all one way."

After his thirty-minute speech, he was welcomed by cheers and applause. In the audience of over 300 were big-name industrialists Henry Flagler and J.P. Morgan. The cotton mills were moving South, bringing the mills to the cotton fields. The time was ripe. While there had been cotton mills pre–Civil War, the textile mill era in the South had begun.[58]

E. Culpepper Clark gives credit to the competent communicator Grady: "The south's gradual, but remarkable recovery from the Civil War was partly due to Grady's one-man campaign to bring prosperity to the region."

Grady stayed in New York to generate support for the South. While there, he befriended General William Tecumseh Sherman. Grady interviewed Sherman and even got him to contribute to a venture that would push forward his New South agenda. Sherman gave $1,000 to the exposition project that Grady promoted. While Grady was the marketer, the idea of bringing the world to Atlanta came from Edward Atkinson.

In 1880, Atkinson wrote an article for a New York journal. In it, he discussed the wasteful handling of cotton and then shipping it north. He suggested an industrial cotton exposition to share ideas and new processes. The *Atlanta Constitution* reprinted the article.

Atkinson was from Boston and New York and knew that bringing mills to the cotton field was not enough. He knew an exposition could change things. He also knew that Atlanta did not have the money to set this in motion. Hannibal I. Kimball was a city builder. He owned the famous Kimball

Hotel. In 1879, he opened the first cotton mill in Atlanta. Kimball invited Atkinson to Atlanta to start the discussion.

When Atkinson arrived, Atlanta influencers asked him to the state senate. On October 28, 1880, Atkinson convinced Georgia senators to bring a cotton exposition to Atlanta. A committee with A.H. Colquitt and Mayor W.L. Calhoun created an organization to incorporate. In February 1881, the chamber of commerce organized and received a charter. Talk is one thing, but this required funds.

The original corporation fixed the capital stock at $100,000 in $100 shares. H.I. Kimball was the fundraising chair and visited northern cities for financial support. He visited New York and secured subscriptions for 253 stock shares worth $25,300. While Boston took 60 shares, Baltimore took 48 shares in the Atlanta Exposition. At the same time, Norfolk, Virginia, bought 25 shares. Philadelphia invested in 43 and Cincinnati 79. The capital stock doubled as the rest of the country and foreign countries became interested. The venue and scope morphed into an international cotton event. With little time, the organizers had much work to do.

The organizers of the first exposition included these Atlanta leaders: Alfred H. Colquitt, Joseph E. Brown, Rufus Bullock, Alfred H. Colquitt, and the Inman brothers. Samuel M. Inman was a cotton broker, and his brother John was wealthy. Grady tagged these wealthy men as those who could rescue the South and Atlanta from financial fragility. Excitement filled the sultry southern air as the committee planned the 1881 International Cotton Exposition.

Chapter 8

THE 1881 INTERNATIONAL COTTON EXPOSITION

C olonel B.W. Wrenn had a great idea. His contribution hides in history. Found in a folder at the Kenan Research Center was a crumbling obituary dated February 9, 1912:

> *With the exception of Henry W. Grady, Colonel Wrenn was the first to see the great future of Atlanta, and while he was general passenger agent of the Western and Atlanta railway he boosted the Atlanta exposition as its secretary and he used printers' ink with great effectiveness. It was he who conceived the idea of a cotton field in the exposition ground and from it was picked, ginned, spun and woven into cloth and then made into a suit of clothes enough of the product for the late Governor Alfred Colquitt, who wore it at the exposition. Colquitt was governor at the time. The whole transaction was done within the day.*[59]

Governor's Day, October 27, 1881, was remarkable. The 1881 International Cotton Exposition was nearing its close when the organizers had a surprise. Some, including original organizer Atkinson, felt southern heat would slow mill production. The planners planned a demonstration of southern pluck.

All thirty-eight governors were invited to Atlanta on this day. (Remember, there were only thirty-eight states in 1881.) Only six attended, but Georgia governor Colquitt led the way. He arrived on the exposition grounds early in the morning for suit measurements.

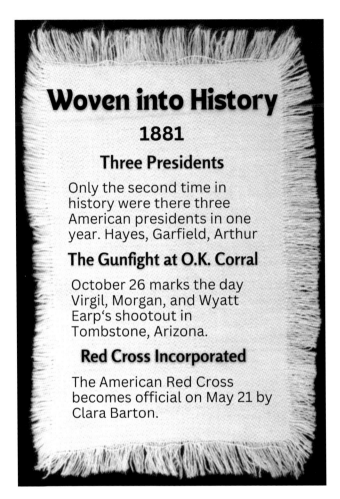

Created by Lisa M. Russell. Photo 15016031 by Valery Kraynov, Dreamstime.com.

The exposition had cotton growing in several plots from several countries. Workers and a machine picked the cotton growing in the patches on the Oglethorpe site. As the sun was coming up, the just-picked cotton was taken to the primary mill and a Compton loom. Millworkers took the cotton, carded it and then spun it. After weaving it, the operatives dyed the cloth black. A seamstress cut the new fabric and sewed it into two suits. At the evening reception, the southern governor and a northern governor wore new swallow-tailed black suits. Clark remarked, "Attendees were astonished Grady was vindicated—from field at dawn to formal attire at dusk, mill to cotton indeed."[60]

In less than one year, the organizers opened the exposition. On October 4, 1881, Governor Colquitt unveiled a beautiful mural by J.H. Moser. "The New South Welcoming the Nations of the Earth was the thesis statement for the first cotton exposition in Atlanta." No one can find images of this banner, but many newspapers described it. In the center of the banner was an attractive brunette girl with the American flag wrapped around her shoulders. One hand pointed toward the exhibits. The other hand was on a bale of cotton. Above her, Uncle Sam welcomed visitors. Columbia was in the background, displayed with a smile of approval. Clio had a pen ready to keep a record of this special event. The image also included African Americans in a cotton field picking the staples.[61]

Atlanta's first exposition was held for two and a half months, from October 4 to December 31. The receipts for paid attendance and sales were between $220,000 and $250,000. Attendance was lower than expected. Approximately 350,000 people attended from thirty-three states and seven countries. Atlanta had a population of 40,000. The highest admission day was December 7, Planters' Day, when 10,293 attended.

They held the exposition in Oglethorpe Park, outside town. The Western and Atlantic trains ran every fifteen minutes to the exposition grounds, what is now Ashby Street in western Atlanta. This area is now in the middle of Atlanta, but it was out in the country at that time.

"The Atlanta International Cotton Exposition." From *Harper's Weekly*, October 15, 1881. *L1981-07_04, 19th and Early 20th Century Labor Prints, Southern Labor Archives. Special Collections and Archives, Georgia State University.*

Organizers constructed the main building as a cotton factory in the shape of a Greek cross. Along the southern side, the agricultural annex had patches of cotton growing from different regions. They annexed the mineral and woods department on the western end. Other important buildings, as reported in a *Georgia Historical Quarterly* article by Stephen K. Prince, were:

> *Railroad building, 200x100 feet*
> *Railroad annexes, 40x60 and 40x100 feet*
> *Agricultural implement building 96x288 feet*
> *Carriage annex, 96x212 feet*
> *Art and industry building, 520x60 feet*
> *Judge's hall, 90x120 feet*
> *Horticultural hall, 40x80 feet*
> *Restaurant, 100x200 feet*
> *Other buildings included the Florida building, press pavilion, police headquarters, and exhibitor booths.*

In 1882, the organizers sold the mill area and opened Exposition Cotton Mills.[62]

Chapter 9

THE 1887 PIEDMONT EXPOSITION

Atlanta, Ga., October 10—No fairer weather or more auspicious circumstance could have attended the opening of the great Piedmont Exposition.

The *New York Times* published this announcement on October 11, 1887. The description of the day continues:

The halls were filled with displays from the tropics, from field and from mine, and the work of art vied with the fertility of nature in lending variety to the scene. The department of machinery was especially well filled, while the poultry show was equal to the best ever seen in the South. The displays of merchandise were abundant. Huge blocks from the manganese, marble, and other mines gave evidence of the character of the raw material in the Piedmont country, while the manufactured articles showed that home work was solving the problem of saving money made in the mines. In the main hall were displayed magnificent specimens of Atlanta woodwork.

Thousands of people thronged through the halls all day long, admiring the display.

Samuel J. Randall opened the exposition. Former Pennsylvania congressman Samuel Jackson Randall spoke about customs. He explained what he would like to do if he were a "maker of customs." Randall was a defender of protective tariffs designed to assist help domestic manufacturers.

When he finished speaking, the *New York Times* reported, "At 3:47 Mr. Randall concluded speaking. Governor [John Brown] Gordon touched an electric button, the signal was given to Gen. [Pierce M.B.] Young, the batteries opened, and to the music of booming cannon the machinery of the great exposition started."

The 1887 Piedmont Exposition, though smaller than the 1881 Exposition, brought visitors and investors to see the latest in cotton and textile production. Some sources described this as part state fair and part cotton exposition. The *Marietta Journal* announced winners of horse races and "blind tigers." In the October 20, 1887 edition, a blurb said, "Among the animals at the Piedmont Exposition last week was the 'blind tiger,' but the prohibitionists made complaint and the blind animal was ejected."

The Piedmont Exposition and the 1895 Cotton States and International Exposition were both held in what is now called Piedmont Park. Pieces of the expositions remain in the park today. In 1887, a small lake was created from a spring that was on the property. Later, in 1895, this lake was enlarged to 11.5 acres and called Clara Meer.

This land was once a forest. When the owners of Piedmont Park tried to sell the property to the City of Atlanta before the expositions, city officials would not buy it. They said the property was too far away from the city. (Today, it is only one mile from downtown.) The city already owned Grant Park and felt there was no need for another city park. It was not until 1904, when the city expanded its limits north, that it finally purchased Piedmont Park.

Dr. Benjamin Walker used this land as his gentleman's farm. In 1887, he sold the land to the Gentleman's Driving Club for horse racing (renamed the Piedmont Driving Club). Piedmont Exposition Company made an agreement with the owners to use the land for fairs and expositions.

A group of men met in the offices of the *Atlanta Constitution* in June 1887. The Piedmont Exposition Company planned the next exposition in three months. The purpose of the Piedmont Exhibition was to exhibit the natural resources in the Piedmont region. Bringing northern dollars south was another motive. An added benefit of the 1887 Exposition was that it would spread electricity across Atlanta.

According to Casey P. Cater in his book *Regenerating Dixie: Electric Energy and the Modern South*, another goal of this exposition was to show off. The exposition directors hoped that the city lights would impress northerners enough to invest in the South. In 1887, Atlanta streets and hotels had electricity. The Piedmont Exposition was lit up for evening events.[63]

"The Piedmont Industrial Exposition at Atlanta—Its Offices and Buildings." From *Frank Leslie's Illustrated Newspaper*, October 22, 1887. *L1981-07_02, 19th and Early 20th Century Labor Prints, Southern Labor Archives. Special Collections and Archives, Georgia State University.*

Organizers included representatives of the North in the programs. Retired Pennsylvania congressman Samuel Jackson Randall gave the opening remarks. New York governor Hall spoke to the crowd on October 12, 1887.

Before his early death at age thirty-nine, Henry Grady helped organize and promote the Piedmont Exposition. The month-long event was smaller and more regional than the 1881 Exposition. On opening day, twenty thousand visitors came. The day of high attendance was when Grady introduced President Grover Cleveland to a crowd of fifty thousand.

President Cleveland came with his wife, Frances Folsom, on October 19. Our twenty-second and twenty-fourth president was the first Democrat elected after the Civil War. He was also part of the 1895 Cotton Exposition. Cleveland was a reformer, serving as Buffalo mayor in 1881 and later as New York governor. In December 1887, right after attending the Piedmont Exposition, he called on Congress to reduce high protective tariffs.

Grover Cleveland was caught on camera walking across the fairground in front of the Georgia building. The main building had a circus tent look and was 570 feet long, 126 feet wide, and two stories high. Images indicate peaks with pennant flags flying over the roof of the main building.

After the exposition closed, civic leaders agreed it had successfully expanded Atlanta's reputation as a place to visit and conduct business. The 1887 Piedmont Exposition set the stage for the larger exposition. The well-marketed Cotton States and International Exposition opened eight years later, in 1895. After the Piedmont Exposition, more of the city was electrified.[64]

Chapter 10

THE 1895 COTTON STATES AND INTERNATIONAL EXPOSITION

Henry W. Grady died on December 23, 1889. He would not be part of Atlanta's most extended, well-publicized, and best-attended exposition. Grady's New South DNA was all over the event. In the official guide, his quote was prominent: "The best reforms of this earth come through waste and storm, and doubt and suspicion."

Times were not easy in 1895, and these words were prophetic.

Walter G. Cooper, chief of the Publicity and Promotion Department, authored *The Official Guide to the Cotton State and International Exposition* in 1896. He explained (in his turn-of-the-century rambling narrative) what the world was like in 1895:

> *It was an inspired audacity which proposed and projects a new enterprise…*
> *in a region not densely populated, without the assurance of government aid,*
> *with no capital subscribed, and in the worst period of depression following*
> *a panic without parallel in the history of the country. When all financial*
> *institutions were carrying heavy loads, when most of the railroads were in*
> *the hands of receivers, and when the average business man was engaged in*
> *a hand to hand conflict with insolvency, the proposition to raise a large sum*
> *by popular subscription for a public enterprise appeared to be the essence*
> *of folly.*[65]

Despite the challenges, the 1895 Cotton States and International Exposition opened on September 18, 1895, with a marching band and

Booker T. Washington gives a controversial speech at the 1895 Exposition. *Courtesy of Library of Congress.*

keynote speeches. John Philip Sousa wrote "King Cotton March" for the exposition. President Grover Cleveland opened the exposition remotely by flipping an electric switch in his Massachusetts home.

African American educator Booker T. Washington delivered his famous "Atlanta Compromise Speech." Washington, once a slave, pulled himself up and founded Tuskegee Institute. He came from a different place, and his methods may seem condescending. His "Gospel of the Toothbrush" was to teach former slaves to enter polite society. A toothbrush was a requirement for admission to his institute. His unique requirements had a purpose. He felt former slaves needed to learn how to adapt. His speaking was controversial, even in his day.

Washington did not challenge the prevailing ideas of segregation. Instead, he urged Black people to make progress as agricultural and industrial laborers. He argued the races could be "as separate as the fingers, yet one as the hand in all things essential to mutual progress."

The Atlanta region had a population of 75,000. Still, between September 18 and December 31, 800,000 visitors came to town from all states and a few countries. The purpose of this exposition changed slightly from the two previous fairs. Exhibiting the products and resources of the southern cotton states was the theme.

The fairgrounds were elaborate, with eleven exhibition buildings full of six thousand exhibits. The primary buildings included the sixty-five-thousand-square-foot U.S. Government Building, the Women's Building, the Georgia Building, the Negro Building, and the Electrical Building. These venues celebrated these groups' accomplishments and touted the day's technological advancements.

The Old Plantation, exhibit at the Cotton States Exposition, Atlanta, Georgia, 1895. *Library of Congress, LC-USZ62-28036.*

The attractions differed from previous expositions. There was a Ferris wheel, a movie theater, water rides, Buffalo Bill's Wild West Show, and a Georgia-versus-Auburn football game. Even the Liberty Bell made its way south. There was a reunion of Confederate and Union soldiers. And night after night, the exposition sky was filled with lights and fireworks.

A reporter was excited about electricity at the exposition as he explained, "Tonight the exposition grounds will be a blaze of glory, and the fair lights darted back and forth among the buildings like fiery serpents. Everything will be weird in the peculiar glow." He described an electric fountain in Lake Clara Meer as a "rainbow of the night." A writer for the *Nation* magazine explained that the electricity "produced a fine artistic effect and the general effect is fairy-like."[66]

Turning Piedmont Park into an exhibition required vast sums of money and unending labor. A sad commentary of the times was the use of convict labor. The *Official Guide* reports in chapter 4, "To this work, the County Commissioners contributed chain gang labor for nearly a year." The *Official*

Guide justifies the use of convicts by saying, "In Georgia it has been found better to put them to work on the public roads than to let them lie in jail, where they become victims of disease." So it was that they came to work at the exposition. It was estimated that this free labor saved the exposition $100,000, which could be put toward skilled labor to build the venue.[67]

The timing might have been better. The region was economically depressed, and the Cotton States Exposition had constant financial problems. After the event, the 1895 Exposition buildings were torn down so the materials could be sold for scrap.

PART IV

FULTON BAG AND COTTON COMPANY

Chapter 11

JACOB ELSAS

"Hey! Put that down! Let me get that for you." Store owner Jacob Elsas stopped another soldier from reaching over his counter and helping himself to his merchandise without paying. He had plans to stop that in his new store.

His first store was an abandoned cabin in Cartersville, Georgia. The tiny space was full of everything a local could use at the tail end of the war and after Sherman marched through town. Jacob knew they would need things. He knew how to get things and how to make money buying inexpensive or repurposing scrap.

His new store in downtown Cartersville would solve the grabby customer problem. With tall counters made of roughhewn lumber, they would have to ask or climb on the counter.

This story comes from a strange document found in the Georgia Tech Archives, a combination play script/blueprint/commemorative booklet. Produced in October 1912, it might have been part of a retirement program for Jacob Elsas, who retired from Fulton Bag and Cotton Company but stayed involved until his death.

This booklet describes how Jacob got his real start in successful business in the North Georgia town of Cartersville. Someone wrote the text like a screenplay on blueprint paper (blue with white print with illustrations of buildings). The tone is that of a major suck-up. The point of the document was to honor Jacob Elsas as the builder of things, the "Master Builder." It starts with the humble cabin. From this document:

Prologue:
Exterior of a small log cabin, through the open door of which is seen rows
of shelving loaded with goods as in a store. Just within the cabin door is a
rough board counter five feet high.

A dialogue between a "soldier" and a "carpenter" ensues. Though it is not clear who the "carpenter" is, it might be Elsas's right-hand man, Mose, an African American who stayed with Elsas for years. The message is clear: he is not going back north, and he loves his boss: "This Georgia air just suits me fine. I've got a job that's great. And soon they'll need more carpenters for all those houses in Atlanta."

The "soldier" continues to press the "carpenter": "You've boasted more about your boss than of this Georgia air. Who is he anyway?"

The "carpenter" answers, "He runs this store, but he'll move out of here soon as the new one's done. I wish he'd sell it out and go to building. Make me his foreman. We could make things hum. He thinks ahead of everything. He plans for special uses and hits it right."

The "carpenter" explains how when he first came to town (Cartersville) there was no lumber, so his boss borrowed the sidewalk planks to build shelves and a counter. He describes how his boss would salvage things to sell and buy other stock up north cheap.

Jacob Elsas's design of a post–Civil War general store in downtown Cartersville, Georgia. In an unusual document honoring Elsas at retirement is this blueprint drawing of the inside of his store. "But look at yonder counter. It's rough as any old board fence." He built a high counter because "some soldiers grabbed his stock and then wouldn't pay. Sometimes a tough would grab at him unless he showed his gun." *Courtesy of Georgia Tech Archives and Special Collections.*

The "carpenter" continues his praise of his boss:

> *He can make a success of anything he starts. But I'm convinced that he's especially cut out for building....No matter what else he does, he's bound to keep on building. It's in his blood. Besides, he does it well. I guess he'll start a factory. His talents lie that way. But, nevertheless he'll keep on building. Perhaps a mill or two. I can almost see his works, fine buildings made to last. He wants what he wants and he gets it. Every detail just his way. A Masterful Builder, I call him and so many others will say.*

And build he did. First, he had to move to Atlanta.[68]

FROM A FAMILY OF WEAVERS

Jacob Elsas was born Elsass in 1842 in the Kingdom of Württemberg, which is in the old German Empire. His family situation is unclear. Some places say he was an orphan, while others say he was born out of wedlock; regardless, it was clear he was on his own at an early age.

He moved in with an uncle and went to school in Ludwigsburg, a prominent southern city in the kingdom. When not in school, he worked for his uncle to pay for his keep. The family wove cotton into bed ticking on handlooms. On the weekends, he would ride the family wagon into the countryside to sell the bed ticking. The family of weavers moved from hand looms to manufacturing. His older brother Isaak immigrated to the United States and changed his family name to Elsas.

Jacob was almost eighteen and feared the draft, so he saved his earning to pay his passage to America. He was nineteen when he crossed the Atlantic Ocean.[69]

Once in New York, he realized he was one dollar short for passage to Cincinnati to see his uncle. His uncle, also named Jacob Elsas, was a successful merchant in Ohio. A fellow traveler of similar age with more money loaned him the cash.

When he got to Cincinnati, young Jacob learned English while he worked as a packer. Learning the language allowed him to sell in neighboring states. The year was 1864, and the Civil War was near its end when twenty-two-year-old Jacob traveled to Nashville, Tennessee, for business.

Some reports suggest Elsas joined or was drafted into the Union army. Further research and using military records, family members will testify

Left: Where it all began. Jacob Elsas, Fulton Bag and Cotton Company founder, after the Civil War in his store in Cartersville, Georgia. *Courtesy of Georgia Tech Archives and Special Collections.*

Opposite: Southern Bag Manufactory poster, 1872. *Courtesy of Jacob Elsas and the Patch.*

that this is fabrication. He went south to sell merchandise. He went to the regional hub and commercial center in Nashville.

Federal troops occupied Nashville. Jacob was scrappy. He bought up woolens he found stored in a flooded warehouse. This purchase wiped out his savings. Elsas was then determined to get a pass to Georgia. Passes were difficult to get, but in 1865, Jacob secured a pass to Dalton, Georgia.

Prince Salm-Salm (Prince Felix Constantin Alexander Johann Nepomuk of Salm-Salm) was the Federal officer in charge in Dalton. He had the town locked down and ordered anyone not in the army or from the area to leave town. They forced Elsas back to Nashville. Then he met Brigadier General Thomas, who offered a pass for him to return to Georgia. He

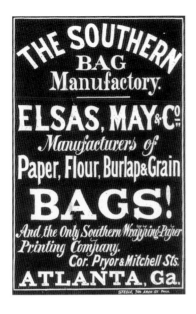

traveled to Cartersville and was allowed to stay.

Elsas found a log cabin that was once a school, and he established a country store. He had merchandise shipped from Cincinnati and Nashville. Jacob made various friends in town, including Judge Milner. Milner was a "very large and heavy southern gentleman with an expansive mansion. He helped young Jacob settle."

Sutlers were civilian merchants attached to armies. They sold items to soldiers out of tents, wagons, or remote outposts. Sometimes the danger was not from battle, but from rogue soldiers or errant officers. In Cartersville, Colonel Adams tried to mess with Elsas's store. Someone intervened (maybe Judge Milner), and Adams left Jacob and his country store alone.

Jacob was not satisfied with the small log cabin, and after a brief time, he had enough money to buy a prime piece of downtown property. He built the first brick store in the center of Cartersville. Cartersville would hold this ambitious entrepreneur down. In 1867, he sold his store and moved to Atlanta.

At auction in 1869, he bought an old market from the city at the corner of Mitchell and Pryor Street. As a merchant, he saw the need for bags to hold merchandise. He bought sewing machines and cloth and began making his own cotton bags. Bags at the time were scarce. The ones you could find were not of standard quality. Elsas started making his quality bags for other merchants who kept ordering without sample but by requesting "the same as last."

Elsas had to buy finished cloth from New England. It made little sense to him to buy cloth from northern textile mills when the cotton was grown in Georgia. He created his own cotton mill and started making his own cloth for his bags.

Jacob Elsas found partners and organized the firm of Elsas, May & Company. The partners bought ten acres near the Georgia Railroad and Oakland Cemetery. Elsas, May and Company bought a corporate charter (difficult to get from the state legislature) from Hannibal I. Kimball. He was not interested in another cotton mill, as his 1879 Atlanta Cotton Factory was

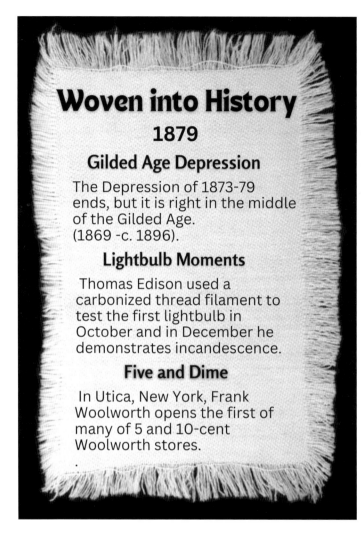

Woven into History

1879

Gilded Age Depression

The Depression of 1873-79 ends, but it is right in the middle of the Gilded Age. (1869 -c. 1896).

Lightbulb Moments

Thomas Edison used a carbonized thread filament to test the first lightbulb in October and in December he demonstrates incandescence.

Five and Dime

In Utica, New York, Frank Woolworth opens the first of many of 5 and 10-cent Woolworth stores.

Left: Created by Lisa M. Russell. Photo 15016031 by Valery Kraynov, Dreamstime.com.

Opposite, top: Fulton Bag and Cotton Company's secondhand bag promotion, 1914. *Courtesy of Jacob Elsas and the Patch.*

Opposite, bottom: Fulton Bag and Cotton sketch, 1940s. *Southern Labor Archives. Special Collections and Archives, Georgia State University, Atlanta.*

not his only priority. In 1880, the partners began a few thousand spindle mills on a Civil War iron foundry. The foundry was destroyed and leveled before the Union army invaded. The property is unique, with an underground water supply to power the mill.

Eventually, the partners separated. May continued the paper bag portion of the business on Pryor Street. Jacob moved to the cotton mill to incorporate. The new corporation was known as Fulton Cotton Spinning Company, later known as Fulton Bag and Cotton Mills.

In the middle of his spinning, Jacob married Clara Stahl in 1870. He met Clara, "a young lady fresh from Rheinsfalz, Germany, while on business

Cash in NEW YORK, 191

Your accumulation of SECOND-HAND BAGS.

We buy them, and pay highest market prices.

Make us an offer or we will make you one.

Use attached card.

Respectfully,

FULTON BAG & COTTON MILLS,

No. 236 Spring St.,

New York, N, Y.

We manufacture New Burlap and Cotton Bags in any size or quality.

THIS SIDE OF CARD IS FOR ADDRESS ONLY

FULTON BAG & COTTON MILLS,
236 SPRING STREET,
NEW YORK, N. Y.

Jacob Elsas at an older age. *Courtesy of Jacob Elsas and the Patch.*

in New York City. They settled in a large home in Atlanta and had six sons and two daughters. Clara died in January 1905."[70]

Jacob Elsas was busy, even after he retired in 1914 and turned the business over to his son Oscar. But he made a daily commute to his Fulton Bag office for twenty years. Retirement was just not in his DNA.

He was a founder and supporter of many Atlanta institutions, such as Atlanta Water Works, Grady Hospital, West View Cemetery, and the Hebrew Orphans' Home. He brought industrial education to the state by helping start Georgia Tech, and he helped establish the Grand Opera House. Until his death, he was a builder.

He died on March 5, 1932. Even in death, he stayed close to his mill. They buried him in Oakland Cemetery.

Chapter 12

OSCAR ELSAS

O scar Elsas was nothing like his father. His father was a builder, and Oscar was a manager. As one of eight children, Oscar was almost ten when Jacob sent his son overseas for two years of school in Stuttgart and then to Boston Latin School for his secondary education. Then his father sent him to the best industrial management schools, first MIT and then transferring as a junior to Georgia Institute of Technology in the first class.

He learned management but did not have the same qualities as his father. In a promotional piece reprinted for a seventy-fifth-anniversary brochure, R.T. Beatty wrote about the Elsas sons, "All the sons were grounded in the principle that industry was created to serve man, and not that man should serve industry. Employees were encouraged to become partners in the business, on the principle that where their investments were, there their hearts and chief interest would be also."

Considering what happened when Oscar took over Fulton Bag, one might call this fake news. Some of the country's biggest textile strikes happened under Oscar's watch.[71]

He became the vice president of Fulton Bag and Cotton after graduating from Tech in 1891. He handled all aspects of plant operations. In 1914, he took over from his father as president. The way he ran things was all about the modern principle of scientific management. This was clear in the way he handled child labor.

In 1906, the Georgia Child Labor Committee, supported by organized labor, tried to push the state's first child labor law. Most mill owners and managers tried to get around these efforts. Oscar felt child labor was substandard and would not hire young children unless the situation was dire. He stated, "Children do not, as a rule, enter our employ as soon as they are of legal age. By 1914, workers sixteen and younger made up only 12 percent of the labor force at Fulton Bag, much lower than the Georgia average."[72]

Oscar seemed a little conflicted about children when he promoted hiring entire families. Fulton Bag had a standing advertisement for "complete families." He said, "We prefer families; they are more reliable for continuous service." He offered tenements in the Factory Lot, just south of the mill. Other low-rent housing was available from the company, but the standards were low.[73] Many Fulton workers lived outside of company housing. The mill district was unsanitary from overcrowding. While Fulton Bag paid more than most textile mills, the officers did not understand that people wanted more than good pay but good living conditions as well. Elsas, true to his nature, blamed it on the work residents.

A 1911 Senate report on working-class life in U.S. cities found that the Fulton County district showed a lack of pride. It mentioned the furniture was "scanty and poor and not arranged for the best effect."[74] Elsas said his company was doing everything possible to improve conditions. "In fact," he said, "more than can be expected of any landlord. He said the workers didn't appreciate it and did not want anything more." He continued, "And when we try to help them, they think we are trying to make money out of them."[75] Oscar Elsas was outspoken about the character of his workers.

Oscar explained that his workforce was transient. "The help is drawn largely from the mountain section of Georgia. Like in the North Georgia cotton mills, most workers came off the farm and worked on the mill floors." Many of the Fulton millworkers moved around and took jobs at other mills. Elsas labeled them as having a "roving and migratory disposition." One Fulton Bag weaver worked in twenty-eight different Georgia and South Carolina mills.[76]

Elsas prided himself on paying the highest wages of any in the state or, "in fact, in the South."[77] His figures for wages paid to workers were accurate, but they also had production fines for substandard work or broken machinery. They also paid higher for store-bought goods that often came out of their pay. Fulton had hidden fines that ate away at the weekly pay envelope.

Oscar was proud of his progressive machinery and new scientific methods of production. He believed efficiency was everything in every area. There was a sizeable clerical staff that kept accurate records. His office staff was

Fulton Seamless bag sample with FBC logo. *Courtesy of Jacob Elsas and the Patch.*

unusually large for the textile industry. He could keep a close eye on all his workers by keeping meticulous records. Later, these records were discovered in the mill's basement when it was to be sold in 1980. Most of these records live in the Georgia Tech archives. Though they seem like minutiae, they say a lot about the management style of Oscar Elsas.[78]

Oscar Elsas created burdensome contracts for new employees. They had to give two weeks' notice to quit or else they lost that entire pay period. Disgruntled employees or unions did not sway him. His resolve was strong, even when interrogated by the government. He said, "This is my business, and I have the right to run it my own way."[79]

This attitude and the labor struggles are further exposed when he was confronted with violence during the strikes. He said, "In an acute situation where I had only men to deal with, I'd just as soon get guns and mow 'em down as not."[80]

The records Oscar left behind after his sudden death in 1924 reveal the reason for the way he handled labor and how it may have led to the 1914–15 strike. He was vengeful against perceived enemies and clung to the reins of control.

Chapter 13

STRIKES, SPIES, AND ESPIONAGE

She was shaking. Her hands were damp with fear of being discovered. They had hired her as a professional mole and operative; Oscar Elsas and company hired her to spy on her fellow workers. She walked past her workstation and dropped the folded handwritten note at the drop site. Her report was full of surveillance that she had recorded that week as she pretended to be just another transient worker in the Fulton Bag and Cotton mill. They paid her extra besides her normal wages for "special projects." Like many of the shady operatives, she worked for a time, got paid, and left town before anyone knew what she was doing.

Oscar Elsas first hired a Pinkerton agent and was later persuaded by a detective agency out of Philadelphia, the Railway Audit and Inspection Company, to hire agents within a few weeks of the strike outbreak. Only Oscar Elsas and general manager Gordon Johnson knew the identities of the ten undercover operatives infiltrating the union and working in the mills.

Here are some examples of the "special work reports" left by spies hired by Oscar Elsas to break the United Textile Workers of America (UTW) and report on workers even after the strike of 1914–15 was over:

Report of Operative #226
Thursday, June 26, 1919

I reported to the Mill the afternoon at 1:00 o'clock and was put to work weaving in #1 Mill

I find the people very friendly, but my loom fixer has a rather stubborn disposition toward the new help, although he may prove to be all right after further investigation. Judging from the looks of things, they are of the demanding kind.

I find my task very hard as a Draper weaver but hope to prove successful. I am putting my whole thought toward this work, so you see I haven't had time to get much information yet. The loom fixers seem to take an interest in their work, and the weavers also.

Report of Operative #115
Friday, July 24, 1914

Attended union meeting at 10:00 A.M. No prayers and no singing to-day. Smith [O. Delight Smith] only speaker. Usual vilification, which I omit, as it becomes nauseating to hear and read of. This woman's personality is disgusting. Noticeable feelings of gloom in meeting. Meeting very flat and uninteresting.

Report of Operative G.J.M.
Wednesday, July 15, 1914

I reported for work at the mill at 6:10 A.M. weighing waste. During the day, I was talking to Mr. Clay. I asked him what he thought of the Union by this time. He said that it was about done, and he knew it would never amount to a damn, and it was just composed of a lot of ignorant people that did not know what they wanted. Later I talked to Mr. Heardy, I asked his opinion of the Union. He said, "h---, that damn thing is one of the past. Them people are just out of a job, so don't let anybody on the outside tell you there's a strike in this mill, for we have all the hands we need here, outside of a few weavers, and I don't think the Company cares much either."

This is what Fulton Bag and Cotton Company came to be under Oscar Elsas, but that was not his father's way. Jacob was the entrepreneur, the industry leader, and the visionary. But his son, MIT and Georgia Tech trained, was the cut-and-dry manager.

TWO 1897 MINI-STRIKES

Before Oscar took over, Jacob hired twenty Black women to sort and fold bags. Cotton mills did not hire Black people, especially women, for production jobs. They had the lowest-paying and most demeaning work in the mill, if they could get in at all. They were the sweepers, cotton cleaners, and truck drivers. Less than 2 percent of textile workers were African American until 1965. So, when Jacob Elsas hired these women, he was not interested in race relations; he wanted workers to fill these new positions. He was not replacing white women but adding jobs. They were not even working in the same area; they were segregated. On August 4, 1897, the white folders walked off the job. Fourteen hundred others joined the women in protest, shutting down the mill.

The Atlanta police were called, forcing Jacob Elsas to fire the Black workers. He slowly increased his Black working population. According to Tiffany Harte for the Atlanta History Center, "The mill resumed hiring Black women by 1900, and by 1914, they made up 11% of the factory's workforce. Just four years later, in 1918, the mill was the largest employer of Black women in Atlanta."[81]

Jacob did not fire the strike leaders right away, but weeks later, he did. This started another strike. On December 7, 1897, most of the company's 1,200 workers went on strike. They wanted assurances they would not have lower wages or be replaced by Black workers. Elsas refused to rehire the strikers and instead shut down the mill and locked striking workers out. He then evicted the strikers from the mill village homes. This short strike ended in January 1898. The union fell apart after the weavers tried to strike later that year.

In September 1911, Ernest Metzger emigrated from Germany and was hired by Jacob Elsas to be an assistant superintendent of his mills. The loom fixers resented his management, as he knew nothing about looms. On Saturday, October 18, 1911, Fulton Mills loom fixer William Fowler told Ernest Metzger to stay off his loom. Later, Oscar Elsas told an *Atlanta Constitution* reporter, "Fowler told him, in vile language, to leave his section and not come back here again." The newspaper said Fowler all but assaulted Metzger. Fowler was fired.

Workers reported a different story. They said that Metzger, not Fowler, flew into a rage. Led by loom fixers on Monday, October 20, 1911, most of the male workers in Mill #2 walked out. Elsas said fixers not only cut off all the looms in the weave room but also ran through the plant stopping machines in other departments and threatening other workers bodily harm if they did not go along. Elsas called the police.

Ten mounted officers arrived and arrested the loom fixers and spinners. They arrested ten workers for disorderly conduct; they were fined. One skipped town and did not appear. One worker made a speech about mill management. This mini strike ended on October 23 when workers met with Elsas, who refused to rehire Fowler. He would not fire the assistant superintendent, Metzger, and he required an internal investigation before reinstating the other workers. The company agreed that a rule requiring six days' pay be withheld revert to five, and by the end of week, they had all returned to work.[82]

Things were just heating up. Workers were unionizing and even had songs to advance the cause. Elsas had informants report this song lyric, to the old tune "How Dry I Am":

> *I'll pawn my hat*
> *I'll pawn my shoes*
> *Before I'll work for a crowd of Jews*

Antisemitism was against the mill owner. Racism and white supremacy were tactics of the union when it helped their cause. The perfect labor storm was brewing.

Life in the mill community was overcrowded and unsanitary. A 1911 Senate report on American cities stated the Fulton district showed few signs of "house pride." The homes had no living rooms and poor sanitary conditions, with no hope of a future outside poverty. Mill manager Oscar Elsas blamed the conditions on the workers, whom he felt had no ambition and were not interested in better. He felt the intense suspicion of mill management had stopped improvements. The workers wanted the mill out of their homes and their lives.

The company doctor would make visits when a worker was sick. Workers felt this was an intrusion. When the company opened a hotel to offer meals for the workers to eat during the day, they refused to go. They would instead take their lunch and find a secluded place to eat. So the meals were discontinued.

The Wesley Settlement House took over the activities once conducted by the mill, and they expanded because the mill was not part of the running of the house.

The rules at Fulton Bag were the worst in the industry. Loom fixers had to deposit a dollar or two, and if their edges were not straight or defect sent the cloth to the seconds pile, they lost their dollars and were fined 20 percent of what the seconds sold for. When they left, they had to give two weeks' notice, or they would lose pay. When a worker left, mill management held back 25 percent of their time until they inspected their work, which could take two weeks.

Turnover was tremendous at Fulton Bag because of these rules. This mill was full of transients and sometimes called the "hobo mill." Millworkers could just go to the other textile mills in town and have fewer rules and no spies. Fulton Bag and Cotton Company and its workers were primed for strikes and union interaction.

Strike of 1914–15

The two previous strikes were tiny preludes to this longer and larger strike that brought the union to town in full force. Harte wrote:

> *Mill workers labored from 6 a.m. to 6 p.m. in Elsas' mill for meager wages. A 1915 report said the average worker could earn up to $20 a week (about $500 a week in 2022). Family units who worked at the mill could earn a little bit more at up to $65 a week. Every morning, they would stroll down the village's narrow streets and shuffle to the factory where they toiled at their machines, pulling, stretching, spinning, weaving, and finishing cotton in intense heat and noise. Overseers ensured that work was done efficiently and to the company's standards and reported unproductive workers to higher-level managers so they could be fined or fired.*[83]

Fiddlin' John Carson, a musician and the most famous of the Fulton Bag strikers, worked in the mill during this time. He was born in Blue Ridge, Georgia, but made the rounds working in mills. He remembered this unsettled time: "In 1913, there was a new word in the mill worker's vocabulary, 'Union.' The Company's position was clear…'NO UNION.'"[84]

Oscar Elsas was in control, and his disposition did not tolerate insubordination. He had just fired a loom fixer who did not give six days' notice. On October 23, 1913, over three hundred loom fixers and weavers performed a work stoppage in protest that lasted for less than a week and led the company to alter its policy on giving notice. They did not rehire the fired workers.

Fulton Bag and Cotton strikers got the attention of the United Textile Workers of America (UTW), a national textile union affiliated with the larger American Federation of Labor (AFL). This union was trying to organize in southern mills. The union membership drive worked, and hundreds of millworkers joined the UTW. The Fulton Bag and Cotton Company became home to UTW Local 886, but the mill did not recognize the union. Instead, they hired spies to infiltrate the unions and spy on workers in the mills.

Oscar had just taken over as mill president when he taunted local union leaders with claims that he had fired three times the number of workers the UTW complained were fired. Elsas would not negotiate, so on May 20, 1914, the highly skilled loom fixers and weavers walked out. They began picket lines. The union workers hoped the strike would end fines, strict contracts and long workdays. They wanted better wages and working conditions. They demanded the end of child labor in the mill.

Elsas called the strike "a little disturbance" and hired workers from other mills. He got workers on loan from the Lindale Mill in Rome, Georgia. Production remained the same, and he evicted striking workers from their homes in Cabbagetown. Workers had no legal right to strike. Gary Fink said, "Textile workers had such a history of losing in the south…. They had to walk out with the assumption they were going to lose."

O. DELIGHT SMITH

The UTW fought hard to support the striking workers and tried to get other workers to join the cause. They provided places to live and eat for the evicted workers, but vagrants (non-union) took over the boardinghouses, tent city, and commissary.

The union leaders used photography to get public support. They photographed Black men evicting families with racial slurs written on the photographs—an attempt to garner white solidarity for the millworkers. They plastered their images in drugstores and made postcards and mailed them across the country, trying to embarrass Oscar Elsas and Fulton Bag.

A progressive Christian organization, Men and Religion Forward Movement, supported the workers and exposed the living conditions in the mill village. On July 7, the group asked the Commission on Industrial Relations to come to Atlanta. Members came and gathered evidence for a week and called hearings and invited Oscar Elsas on July 16. He refused to listen to the commission and refused arbitration. He said he had nothing to negotiate. There was little the commission could do but report to the U.S. Department of Labor, but the mill owners did not want these reports made public.

At the end of July 1914, Elsas said he would never rehire strikers and they would be blacklisted. In August, he declared the strike over. The UTW had financial troubles and was forced to close up shop. After 360 days, the strike ended on May 15, 1915. The strikers had to find new homes and jobs. Though the strike was not a success for workers, the U.S. Commission on Industrial Relations investigation could push for new labor laws. It set the stage for the 1934 textile workers' strike.

From the beginning, the union lost the fight. The mills had too much money and too many strong operatives who would work for extra pay to fight the union. The union leaders were weak, and Elsas preyed on those weaknesses. The leading crusader for the United Textile Workers Union (UTW) was Ola Delight Lloyd Smith, called "O. Delight" or Mrs. E.B. Smith.

O. Delight was a woman out of place in her time. Born on January 21, 1880, she worked as a telegrapher, journalist, and most notably as a labor activist. In the early 1900s, she came to Atlanta, where she wrote for the *Atlanta Journal of Labor* and became the associate editor.

In 1914, she began her work as a leader in the UTW as they organized the strike against Fulton Bag and Cotton Company. She was driven and challenged gender norms of her time. She was not ladylike and had little patience for the second-class citizenship given to women. She resisted her husband's leadership and even refused to carry a baby; she had abortions instead. She physically defended herself with brass knuckles when attacked by company thugs or aggressive men.

Today, we might admire O. Delight Smith's feminist traits and tenacity, but in early twentieth-century southern sensibilities, women did not act like this, and it hurt her cause. Fulton Bag management used her personality against her. Spies followed her around and recorded her every move, and not only in union meetings where she spoke and led the workers.

Her use of photography to provoke public sympathy was stronger than that of her contemporary Lewis Hine. She made postcards and sent them across the country and into the hands of politicians. Her images also differed from Hines's work in tone. She scratched evocative and sometimes untrue captions directly on the negatives. She used racial and exaggerated commentary and then sent them across the country and to politicians.

Mill owners and some union members did not like Smith and accused her of having affairs with her fellow leaders Charles Miles and Pat Callahan.

Four child laborers. *Far left*: Milton Nunley (Nunnally), *far right*: Mel Baldwin. The caption reads, "32c a week, 50c a week, 50c a week." *Photo by Duane A. Russell, L1983-38_16, Fulton Bag and Cotton Mill strike photographs, Southern Labor Archives, Special Collections and Archives, Georgia State University, Atlanta.*

Elsas assigned a former Secret Service agent to follow Miles and Smith to a hotel, where they registered under false names. The agent tried to make a deal with Smith. For his silence about her affair, he suggested a liaison with him. Instead, she promised to set him up with another woman. The woman gave the agent gonorrhea.[85]

Smith's eventual downfall was with Pat Callahan, the UTW's quartermaster. He lived in the tent city set up for the striking workers who had been evicted from their company homes. Smith took every advantage of those evictions and photographed families being thrown out on the street.

Many moved into the tent cities and took advantage of the commissary. Callahan had gotten seriously injured during a weekend brawl in the tent city. O. Delight took Callahan to his home after he got out of the hospital. Her husband, Edgar, was about to lose patience with the patient.

United Textile Workers of America president John Golden in the strike camp during the Fulton Bag and Cotton Mill strike. Also shown is Mrs. E.B. Smith, who worked with the union and collected images for the strike. *L1985-34_140, Labor Photographs, Fulton Bag and Cotton Mill, strike of 1914–15 collection, L1985-34, Southern Labor Archives, Special Collections and Archives, Georgia State University, Atlanta.*

REWARD!

The undersigned will pay the sum of $100.00 reward for proof that will result in arrest and conviction of the person who assaulted Homer Sims, an employee of this Company, on July 25, 1914 about 10:30 P. M. on Decatur St., near Boulevard.

FULTON BAG & COTTON MILLS.

A 1914 "wanted" poster from Fulton Bag and Cotton Mills. *Courtesy of Georgia Tech Archives and Special Collections.*

He came home one day and found Callahan and Smith drunk and half dressed. Mr. Smith moved out and filed for divorce. He got his divorce lawyer with the help of Fulton Bag and Cotton Company, which despised his wife. Mr. Smith charged his wife with conduct "at variance with the duties of a good wife" and claimed that she "wouldn't stay home where all good women ought to be." The judge sided with Edgar Smith and refused her request for alimony. He was given the right to remarry, but she was not.[86]

Even though O. Delight Smith was the leader of the union and strike against Fulton Bag and Company, the members resented her. Spies only stirred the resentment more. R.H. Wright, a millworker who became a union leader, did not care for O. Delight. He complained that non-millworkers were living in the tent city and taking food from the commissary meant for the unemployed strikers. He eventually quit the strike and Fulton Bag and found work elsewhere.

With everyone against her, Smith left town in disgrace. The strike and her marriage fell apart. Yet later, she fondly looked on her two years in Atlanta with the UTW as the best of her life.

UPRISING OF 1934

The uprising of 1934 was not as big as the yearlong 1914 strike at Fulton Bag. Roosevelt's New Deal started this strike.

The 1933 National Recovery Act (NRA) of the Roosevelt administration set new industry-wide standards for wages, hours, and workplace safety, eliminating once and for all child labor for those under sixteen years old. The hourly rate for men working in the mills (no mention of women) was set to thirty cents per hour, and hours were dropped to forty per week. This law applied to all industries, including textile mills.

The 1935 National Labor Relations Act granted workers the right to form unions and strike. Roosevelt's new alphabet gave workers the right to strike without fear of losing their jobs. The NRA required mill operators to follow the rules, and when they did not, workers could organize.

Governor Eugene Talmadge campaigned as the workingman's friend, but he quickly changed his tactics in September 1934. He broke his election promises not to call out the National Guard.

On September 1, 1934, Labor Day, forty-four thousand Georgia textile workers joined the picket lines. This was the beginning of the largest labor strike in the history of the South. This roughly organized protest spread throughout the South and along the Eastern Seaboard, with groups like the Flying Squadron stirring up workers to leave their posts. Violence ensued in a few Georgia mills, and deaths were reported in Trion and Augusta.

Talmadge declared martial law. He ordered National Guard troops to Georgia mills to arrest strikers. They sent the protesters, including women and children, to Fort McPherson, an outdoor former World War I German prisoner-of-war camp, until they could be tried in military court.

Governor Talmadge later said:

> When the national guards are ordered out, they are to protect the lives and property of all of the citizens of this state. This means strikers, union members, non-union members, laborers, executives, and all. I hope that there will not be a skin scratched in the whole state of Georgia. I hope that the citizens of the state will realize the necessity of preserving order. I do not want any interference from parties outside of the state of Georgia. I do not want any imported officers or imported strikers. Peaceful picketing that does not interfere with the rights of any citizen or business will also be protected.[87]

The New Georgia Encyclopedia wrote:

> This General Textile Strike of 1934, later termed the Uprising of '34, involved more than 200,000 northern workers and 170,000 southern workers and was the largest labor protest in the history of the South; approximately 44,000 workers participated in Georgia. Some were drawn out of their factories by "flying squadrons," or caravans of cars filled with workers who traveled between mills and encouraged others to join the strike.

Top: Women strikers, the Flying Squadron. *Courtesy of Special Collections and Archives, Georgia State University, Atlanta.*

Middle: Atlanta strikers with National Guard, 1934. *Courtesy of Special Collections and Archives, Georgia State University, Atlanta.*

Bottom: National Guard escorting women strikers to a former prisoner of war camp. *Courtesy of Special Collections and Archives, Georgia State University, Atlanta.*

National Guardsmen dispersing striking textile workers outside the Fulton Bag, 1934. *LBRE2017-03a, Lane Brothers Commercial Photographers Photographic Collection, 1920–76. Photographic Collection, Special Collections and Archives, Georgia State University Library.*

Strikers at Fulton Bag Company during the 1934 strike. *LBRE2017-04c, Lane Brothers Commercial Photographers Photographic Collection, 1920–76. Photographic Collection, Special Collections and Archives, Georgia State University Library.*

Labor lawyer Joe Jacobs had much to say in his interview for the Uprising of '34 series:

> *There are a lot of things to tell you about the strike of '34. In my mind, that's the closest thing to a revolution that I have seen in this country, and that, by the way, includes even the Civil Rights marches and everything else. And the reason I say that is because it was so spontaneous. Uh, just before that strike was when Roosevelt tried the Blue Eagle of the National Recovery Act, and when he did not keep going, the people who had been led to believe that with his advent that there would be a better day, found that it wasn't. What was happening was because the depression was moving in so strongly, the companies were cutting back. They were increasing workloads. If they had money, they were buying newer machinery, increasing workloads because of the new machinery. And instead of them making more money, they were making less money. And once the strike started, it caught like wildfire. And when I say, "caught like wildfire," it spread everywhere. You did not have the communication systems that we have now, but the grapevine served to do it.*[88]

Chapter 14

CABBAGE TOWN

VILLAGE LIFE THEN

Cabbagetown resident Calvin Freeman talks about Fulton Bag's housing:

> There used to be a row of houses up there they called Chinch Row, and
> everybody wanted to stay away from Chinch Row. Didn't nobody want to
> live in those houses over there because they were full of chinches (Spanish
> for bedbugs). Then they had these other little homes that would handle a
> family of maybe five people. You had a hard time, you know, waiting on the
> list to get a good home to live in.[89]

Cabbagetown began as Factory Town when Jacob Elsas wanted to
provide affordable housing for his workers and their families. In 1881,
factory owners promised white laborers from the hills of northern Georgia
wages and benefits. Elsas built a small community of simple frame one-
and two-story cottages around the mill. No one is sure how the village got
its nickname, but here are a few stories from cabbagetown.com:

> There are many tales and versions of how Cabbagetown, a little Cotton
> Mill Village, got its name. Here are a few:
>   According to Marion A. "Peanut" Brown, when she moved to the
> Fulton Bag and Cotton Mill Village in 1919 she got her first job

peddling produce on foot and carrying baskets of sweet potatoes from door to door. There she met and worked with Joe Newman from a mule-drawn wagon. They peddled around town through the week, but on Fridays and Saturdays many produce wagons would park at one of three different mill gates. They soon found that cabbages sold better than all the other produce and decided to take entire loads of nothing but cabbage, thus the beginning of the name Cabbagetown. She says the name slowly spread and by the mid 1930's the place was well known as Cabbagetown.

Another explanation is the mostly transplanted poor Appalachian residents (largely of Scottish-Irish descent) who worked in the nearby Fulton Bag and Cotton Mill, would grow cabbages in the front yards of their shotgun houses and one could distinctly smell the odor of cooking cabbage coming from the neighborhood. People outside the neighborhood said "Cabbagetown" with derision, but it soon became a label of pride for the people who lived there. A variation of this explanation is that a local cab company operating off Memorial Drive gave nicknames to various neighborhoods they serviced and the specifically called the mill town Cabbagetown, because of the smell.

Yet another explanation is that a train carrying a load of cabbages derailed by the mill adjacent to the neighborhood and the poor residents quickly accumulated the cabbages and used them in just about every meal. A variation of this legend has a Ford Model T taking a sharp turn at one of the main intersections of Cabbagetown, and flipping over spilling its cargo of cabbages across the street. Someone yelled "Free Cabbages!" and they were soon carted away by the residents.

Joyce Brookshire lived in Cabbagetown her whole life. Her mother worked at Fulton Bag and Cotton Mills for twenty-nine years. She is proud of the heritage and community. In the 1990s, she and a group of community members started the Cabbagetown Revitalization effort. They were a land trust that built six new houses on Savannah Street and rehabilitated five original houses from the old factory lot. The mill started selling those homes in the 1950s, mostly to landlords who were not committed to the community. The houses deteriorated. In addition, this group pushed to restore the old mill into low- and moderately priced living spaces. Those plans changed, but the spirit of the original revitalization group remains.

Left: Fulton Bag and Cotton made Jim Dandy cotton bags before production ceased. They display this last bag at Georgia Tech Archives. *Courtesy of Georgia Tech Archives and Special Collections.*

Below: Fulton Bag Company's mill town was called Cabbagetown in the 1940s. *Courtesy of Special Collections and Archives, Georgia State University, Atlanta.*

Opposite, top: Stacks behind cabbage, 1940s. *Southern Labor Archives. Special Collections and Archives, Georgia State University, Atlanta.*

Opposite, bottom: Fulton Bag and Cotton Mill smokestacks in the 1940s. *Southern Labor Archives. Special Collections and Archives, Georgia State University, Atlanta.*

Fulton Bag and Cotton school playground, 1955. *LBCB053-107a, Lane Brothers Commercial Photographers Photographic Collection, 1920–76. Photographic Collection, Special Collections and Archives, Georgia State University Library.*

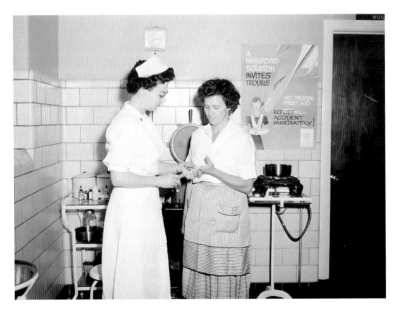

Company nurse at Fulton Bag and Cotton, circa 1950s. *N07-078_c, Tracy O'Neal Photographic Collection, 1923–75. Photographic Collection, Special Collections and Archives, Georgia State University Library.*

Top: This image was part of a series by Lewis W. Hine in 1915. Mrs. Dora Stainers lived in the factory town at Fulton Bag and Cotton Company at 562½ Decatur Street. Dora is thirty-nine years old. She began spinning in an Atlanta mill when she was seven years old. She has worked for Fulton Bag for thirty-two years. Her little girl Lilie is the same age she was when she started work, but the mother says, "I ain't goin to put her to work if I can help it. I'm goin' to give her as much education as I can so she can do better than I did." *Library of Congress Prints and Photographs Division Washington, D.C., March 1915, LC-DIG-nclc-02989.*

Bottom: Mrs. Dora Stainers only had four days of schooling. At seven, she made $0.20 a day. The most she ever made was $1.75 a day, and now she is earning $1.00 a day when she works. She is now looking for a job. *Library of Congress Prints and Photographs Division Washington, D.C., March 1915, LC-DIG-nclc-02984.*

Lewis W. Hine visited Atlanta and the Fulton Bag and Cotton Mills to document child labor abuse in 1915. His images made an impression on Congress that helped eliminate unfair labor practices, especially for children. Georgia did not change its laws until it was forced to by the Roosevelt administration in the 1930s. This is Lilie. She is the same age her mother was when she began working in the mill. *Library of Congress Prints and Photographs Division, Washington, D.C., March 1915, LC-DIG-nclc-02985.*

Early sketch of Fulton Bag. *L1983-38_11, Fulton Bag and Cotton Mill strike photographs, Southern Labor Archives, Special Collections and Archives, Georgia State University, Atlanta.*

The Fulton Bag Company stacks still standing. Image for application to the National Register of Historic Places, 1970s. *Photo credit David Kaminsky. Courtesy of Jacob Elsas and the Patch.*

Cabbagetown image for application to the National Register of Historic Places, 1970s. *Photo credit David Kaminsky. Courtesy of Jacob Elsas and the Patch.*

Multiple family housing built in the old factory town. Image for application to the National Register of Historic Places, 1970s. *Photo credit David Kaminsky. Courtesy of Jacob Elsas and the Patch.*

Cabbagetown mill village in the 1970s. Image for application to the National Register of Historic Places. *Photo credit David Kaminsky. Courtesy of Jacob Elsas and the Patch.*

View north up Reinhardt Street of the apartment houses built for workers in Cabbagetown. Image for application to the National Register of Historic Places, 1970s. *Photo credit David Kaminsky. Courtesy of Jacob Elsas and the Patch.*

Berean Avenue mill village home in Cabbagetown. Image for application to the National Register of Historic Places, 1970s. *Photo credit David Kaminsky. Courtesy of Jacob Elsas and the Patch.*

Kirkwood Avenue mill village home in Cabbagetown. Image for application to the National Register of Historic Places, 1970s. *Photo credit David Kaminsky. Courtesy of Jacob Elsas and the Patch.*

Left: Fulton Mills view from Oakland Cemetery, 1970s. *Courtesy of Jacob Elsas and the Patch.*

Right: Cabbagetown. Image for application to the National Register of Historic Places, 1970s. *Photo credit David Kaminsky. Courtesy of Jacob Elsas and the Patch.*

Fenwick Street in Cabbage Town. *Courtesy of Jacob Elsas and the Patch.*

Brookshire shared a song, "The Cabbage Town Ballad":

We came in 1885 to work in the new cotton mill, for we had heard the pay was good. There were many jobs to fill. We said goodbye to our mountain homes, there to return no more. But we brought with us the way of life that we had known before.

We're a mountain clan called Cabbagetown in the city of Atlanta, GA, and if it be the will of God, it's where we'll always stay.

Sometimes the way was hard to bear. Our lives were never our own. To the owner of a cotton mill your soul to him belongs, when the bad times got us down and good times were so few, we'd sing old songs about our mountain homes, our music would see us through.

We're a mountain clan called Cabbagetown in the city of Atlanta GA, and if it be the will of God it's where we'll always stay.

And now the smokestack smokes no more. No whistle blows at dawn. They've taken all they wanted from us, packed up their cotton and gone. And we are left to live our lives in the world that's never too kind, but the strength of a mountain's in us all and a new day we will find.

We're a mountain clan called Cabbagetown in the city of Atlanta GA, and if it be the will of God it's where we'll always stay.

We're a mountain clan called Cabbagetown in the city of Atlanta GA, and if it be the will of God it's where we'll always stay.[90]

Village Life Now

Along with the mill, the original houses in Cabbagetown made it into the National Register of Historic Places in 1976. After the mill closed in 1977, the village declined. Some original millworkers stayed, but others left and new people moved in, including many artists.

In 1995, as the old neighborhoods in Atlanta went through gentrification, the mill was sold and converted into luxury lofts. Now it sits behind gates as a gated community called Fulton Cotton Mill Lofts.

The mill and the village have suffered fires and a tornado, but the community stuck together and pulled through it all. According to the website for the housing community, "Today, Cabbagetown is home to a unique mix of families, singles, young couples, artists and professionals. Home styles include farmhouse Victorians, bungalows and early 1900's shotgun style homes. It is a rural-type neighborhood community within an urban setting."

PART V

EXPOSITION MILLS

Chapter 15

IT BEGAN AT THE FAIR

A fter the fair was over, Exposition Mills was born. Instead of tearing it all down, the 1881 International Cotton Exposition organizers salvaged the central cross building and created one of the early cotton factories in Atlanta.

Atlanta business executives gathered and moved forward with a new mill. This was a natural continuation of the International Cotton Exposition. On January 10, 1882, weeks after the closing of the exposition, Atlanta mayor James W. English held a meeting in his office. He discussed with organizers the sale of the exposition buildings and land. In that meeting were these Atlanta business owners: Walker P. Inman, Hugh T. Inman, George W. Parrott, Frank P. Rice, Robert H. Richards, William W. Austell, William B. Cox, Evan P. Howell, James H. Porter, Thomas L. Langston, John L. Hopkins, Richard Peters, and J.W. Murphy. The meeting was a success, and it made the news the following day. Franklin M. Garrett writes about Atlanta's history in his volumes *Atlanta and Environs*. From newspaper accounts, he records the beginnings of Exposition Mills:

> *"There are few cities of 40,000 people," said a gentleman yesterday, "in which twenty-five men casually brought together will put up $10,000 each to invest in a manufacturing enterprise. Yet this is exactly what the corporation of the exposition factory has done. And more than this, they could, in an hour, add twenty-five more men to their list who would put up another $10,000 each, or in an hour's session the same stockholders would*

Woven into History

1882

Labor Day Established

First celebrated on Tuesday, September 5 in New York City planned by the Central Labor Union.

The Chinese Exclusion Act

Congress passed the Chinese Exclusion Act, which barred Chinese immigrants from the United States for 10 years.

Electricity Advances

Thomas Edison opens first power station while other inventors produce the first electric iron and fans.

Created by Lisa M. Russell. Photo 15016031 by Valery Kraynov, Dreamstime.com.

agree to double what they have put up. There is plenty of money in Atlanta whenever it is called for legitimately."

The newspaper article continues to explain they were ready to build: "Certainly—there is nothing in the way. The start will be made with ten thousand spindles and looms to match. The boilers and engines are already in place. The mill will be started this year, although much of the machinery will have to be made especially for it."

The newspaper reporters asked about operatives (workers) for the new mill, and officers responded, "We will lodge them in the Exposition Hotel [across the W&A tracks from the exposition grounds proper]. This will be

Exposition loom, 1950s. *N05-167_b, Tracy O'Neal Photographic Collection, 1923–75. Photographic Collection, Special Collections and Archives, Georgia State University Library.*

changed somewhat and will do capitally for operatives. It will accommodate a great many."

The next question was about the extra buildings on the exposition site:

> *They will be put to some good use. You see we have a considerable little village out there, and we shall utilize every bit of it. The general plan is to build up a system of small industries about the great central factory. We may utilize the small buildings and annexes for cotton seed mills, or plants or anything else we think profitable. The company can raise all the capital it needs. Each man has confidence in his colleagues, and there will be no lack of money. The exposition mills will prove to be the most important manufacturing enterprise in or around Atlanta.*

On March 4, 1882, the Superior Court of Fulton County issued articles of incorporation to the Exposition Cotton Mills. They fixed the capital stock at $250,000. The petitioners were Hugh T. Inman, Walker P. Inman, Richard Peters, Robert H. Richards, James Swann, Thomas L. Langston, William

B. Cox, William W. Austell, William J. Garrett, James H. Porter, Robert D. Spalding, J.W. Harle, George W. Parrott, Daniel N. Speer, Robert M. Clark, Lodowick J. Hill, Evan P. Howell, Edward C. Peters, and John D. Turner.

One month later, Hugh T. Inman was the first president of the Exposition Cotton Mills. Conditions were right, and the mills prospered. Miles of yarn and cloth were first produced and sold exclusively to J.P. Stevens & Company, New York.

Chapter 16

IT TAKES A VILLAGE

A caption in 1957's *75ᵗʰ Anniversary Commemorative Publication*, written by the mill, bragged about the mill house remodel: "A house in the mill village before modernization is shown at left. At right is an example of the improved version, complete with brick foundation and asbestos shingles."

Yikes. Asbestos shingles.

Housing was part of the employment package for most cotton mill villages. Not only did the company provide low-cost housing, but it also maintained it. According to a 1969 *Atlanta Journal-Constitution* article, seven hundred of these houses rented for six dollars a week. Mills provided inexpensive and convenient housing for the workers. Besides the savings, workers could walk to work and not pay for transportation.

Exposition Cotton Mill worker Nesbitt Spinks remembered, "The mill village was a great big place; the company owned all the houses, and they'd rent you the houses pretty cheap. I think I paid four dollars and something a month for a three-room house. Of course, all house rent was cheap back then, but that was cheaper than you could get it anywhere else, you know."[91]

They also had a company store: "The store had everything…including everyday clothes.…You could spend all your money…advantages and disadvantages.…As long as you were working, you had a book, and they wrote what you spent, and by Monday you could start over."

Katie Lovins remembered the store and the nursery: "They had a nursery down there. For years there they kept children for the mothers

Above: This streetcar went to Exposition Mills, but it was also used at Whittier Mills for transportation to the mills. *Courtesy of Whittier Mill Village Association.*

Opposite: The *Exposition* was the company newspaper. It reveals life in a lost mill village, 1919. *Courtesy of Atlanta History Center.*

to work in the mill. And the clinic was there. The mill had doctors [for workers]. And they had a company store. They had just about everything, clothes and groceries."[92]

Clifford Lovins remembered the bad side of the company store: "Well, there was a lot of people that worked there I know, that never drawed a dime in money for ten years. The store got it all."

Beyond the physical houses, the village created a community. Images show that Exposition Mill Village was busy. Images from the Atlanta History Center show baseball teams, youth football, bowling leagues, and even indoor swimming. In 1945, there were Halloween fairs and baby contests. They cared for the children in company-owned nurseries, and medical clinics were on site. The mills offered evening classes for employees taught by Atlanta school system instructors.

The *Exposition* newspaper advertised for members and reported on the progress of the Exposition Mills Band. From the March 29, 1937 edition:

PLANT A GARDEN! PREPARE NOW	# THE EXPOSITION	START A SAVINGS ACCOUNT

VOL. 1 — ATLANTA, GEORGIA, FEBRUARY 22, 1919 — NO.

Mr. Glenn Says: Where Is That Base Ball Team?

BAND CONCERT SATURDAY NIGHT

Big Program By Expo Band at Pastime at Seven O'Clock, Sharp

The big event of the winter will take place on the evening of Washington's Birthday, when the famous and well-known Exposition Band will give a concert at the Pastime for the benefit of the organization.

The performance will begin at seven o'clock sharp. Admission will be twenty-five cents for adults and ten cents for children.

Although the band has been heard on several occasions in the past, this is the first time that it has ever been heard in a paid concert, and it has been practicing hard for its initial appearance. A most attractive program has been arranged by the director, W.

There will be vocal solos by Miss Annie Bennett, vocal solos by Miss Eugene Guntharp, a cornet solo by W. D. Guntharp, a trombone solo by Ralph Gerard, a vocal solo by Mrs. Nellie Dees, and last, but by no means least, Jim and Jack Lawson in a fiddling specialty.

With such an array of talent to assist them, the members of the band are obliged to make good on their concert. The soloists alone would be worth the price of admission.

There has been an orchestra organized as well as a band, and the orchestra will play several numbers.

The Pastime management has consented to move its Friday show to Saturday in order to give added interest to the entertainment.

Come one, come all. The Pastime should be packed when the first number begins to play on Saturday evening.

The program is as follows:
March, Royal Welcome Home . . Band.
Fox Trot, Mammy's Little Coal Black Rose . . . . Orchestra
March, R. M. B. . . . . Band
One Step, Loading up the Mandy Lee . . . . Orchestra
Piano Solo, Suwanee River, air varie . . . . Miss Annie Bennett.
Vocal Solo, Till We Meet Again, Miss Eugene Guntharp
Waltz, Belgian Rose . . . . Band
March and Two Step, Our Boys . . . . Orchestra
Cornet Solo, Holy City, W. D. Guntharp
Trombone Solo, Smear Lasses, Ralph Gerard.

Fox Trot, Dark Town Strutters . . . .
March, Spirit of Independence . . . .
Vocal Solo, Selected . . Mrs. Nellie Dees
Serenade, Love's Response . . . . Band
Waltz, Blue Danube . . . . Orchestra
Fiddle Specialty . . Jack and Jim Lawson
Medley . . . . and
Final, Star Spangled Banner . . . . Band and Orchestra.

36 YEARS ON THE JOB!
WONDERFUL SERVICE RECORD

MISSES MARY AND LIZZIE ANDERSON.

Record breakers for length of service at the Exposition Mills are Mary and Lizzie Anderson. Their family came from Roswell in 1883. Mary and Lizzie and their brother and mother. Three, two girls and the boy, went to work in the Exposition Cotton Mills July, 1883. Lizzie has been at work constantly since.

The brother became an efficient weaver and rose from one position to another and is now the Boss Weaver at the Dan River Cotton Mills in Virginia, (the largest Mills in the South). After the death of the mother and the marriage of the brother, Lizzie and the

home and Mary continues in the Mill. They own their own comfortable home on Wheeler Street, paid for from earnings at the Mill. Mary and Lizzie have known personally every Superintendent and President of the Mill since the organization. They feel a personal proprietorship in the Mill. Mary does not want to quit her work and receive a pension, for she says she would not know what to do with herself if she couldn't come to work every day. This July she will have been regularly on the job for 36 years.

The Exposition management appreciates such long and faithful service. It is upon such records that the success of the mill is based.

NOTICE.

Please watch your hydrants and spigots and prevent waste of water. The Mill has to pay for every cubic foot of water used or wasted.

EXPOSITION COTTON MILLS.

TARZAN PICTURE AT THE PASTIME

Marvelous Romance of the African Jungles on Monday

One of the most interesting pictures ever made is "Tarzan of the Apes." This picture has been shown for months in New York and other large cities for two dollars a seat, just the same as a big theatrical show. In Atlanta it was shown for fifty cents.

And now it comes to the Pastime on Monday for the delight and entertainment of the employes of the Exposition Cotton Mills and their friends. No one should miss it. You will regret it if you do.

The scenes in "Tarzan" are laid in Africa. The story tells of a baby . . . . . and how the . . . . . in the jungles, and the . . . it grew into a prodigious giant of a man, stronger than any other man, who at the same time could swing from limb to limb in the tops of the trees just like the apes.

Finally, an English exploring party passed that way and discovered this singular creature. He was finally prevailed upon to make friends, and on one occasion saved the young lady of the party from the lions by taking a lion and tearing him jaw from jaw in one of the most thrilling scenes ever shown in a picture.

At another time, he saves the entire party from the savages, and single handed battles against the whole tribe and defeats them.

All through the picture there are scenes in which the monkeys, apes, lions and other wild beasts of the jungle stalk before the camera as though they were domestic beasts. The pictures of the apes in the woods are nothing short of marvelous. The jungle is pictured in a way that it has never been pictured before.

"Tarzan" is thrilling, exciting, marvelous. It is one of the big pictures of the screen. Be sure that the children see it.

The Pastime for the rest of the week includes Houdini's serial and Charlie Chaplin comedy on Wednesday and an installment of the "Brass Bullet" on Friday. There is something interesting every day.

We, the members of the newly organized Exposition Band wish to extend thanks to the management of the mill for the splendid new instruments they have furnished us. We also thank them for their cooperation in giving time out to members who work on the second shift, so they can attend rehearsals. Our aim is to make this band something the mill management and community will be proud of. We are working hard to make it a success, and in a few weeks we will be able to produce a pretty fair grade of music.[93]

The *Exposition* newspaper showed that the company encouraged church attendance. North Georgia mill owners were more invested; they purchased churches and paid the pastors. At Exposition Mills, the local church had a column. From a 1937 edition of the *Exposition*:

> *News Notes from Jefferson Street Church:*
>
> *Attend some Church*
> *The habit of staying away from church services is being by practiced by a lot of folks today. Every person should go to church somewhere. If you do not already go to church at some place, Jefferson Street gives you a most cordial invitation to all services of worship. Begin next Sunday and form a habit of churchgoing.*

And of course, food was involved. This must have helped the women working in the mills until noon on Saturdays. "Lunches are served each Saturday by ladies of the church from 11 am–9 pm. Six hotdogs or hamburgers for 25 cents."

The *Exposition* had regular columns with gossip and news with unusual headings:

> *Cloth Room Scraps*
> *Spinning Room Yarns*
> *Carding Room Tangles*
> *Weave Room Warps*
> *Shop Shavings*

Exposition Mill workers gave back. In the *Exposition*, you see participation in the March of Dimes with advertisements saying, "Polio isn't licked yet!" and "Infantile Paralysis: It will take more in '54."

The *Exposition* explained the company's history in the 1952 edition. The newspaper writers explained how the mill was born of the 1881 Exposition:

> *Seventy Years Ago*
> *The original grounds were known as Oglethorpe Park and owned by Atlanta city. A large part of the grounds was used as a model cotton plantation where growing specimens could be seen.*
>
> *A large new building in shape of a Greek Cross was built to house the model cotton machinery of the day and was shown during Exposition to*

hundreds of thousands of visitors. The original structure of the 1881 is the nucleus of our present day mill. Many additions have been made on all sides and on top, but the original part is still in use.

One more interesting highlight: James A. Garfield, President of the United States, was to have opened the Exposition in person, but he was assassinated just before it opened.[94]

The *Exposition* recorded the company's war effort. Cotton mills and textile production were essential to the effort. They added cartoons to the *Exposition* as propaganda to encourage workers to work for the boys away fighting.

Two February 1943 editions of the *Exposition* had cartoons touting the use of cotton during war. An image of soldiers in the jungle with ID tags taped had this caption: "How does cotton help 'the boys' in New Guinea outsmart Jap snipers? Soldiers, penetrating enemy lines, tape their metal identification tags with Cotton Adhesive to guard against a betraying noise."

Another had an image of a blimp floating above the ocean with this caption: "How does Cotton help rid the sea lanes of submarines? Answer: Blimps on constant sea patrol duty are made of cotton fabric."[95]

On March 16, 1943, the War Department visited Exposition Mills to give employees the Army-Navy E Award. Production was paramount during World War II. The president said, "Victory depends in large measure on the increased war production we are able to get from our factories and arsenals....This is total war. We are all under fire...soldiers and civilians alike—no one is a spectator. To win we must fight, and to fight we must produce."

The Army-Navy E Award, or the Excellence in War Production Award, encouraged the production of materials needed for the military. The army only gave E Awards to high-quality and high-quantity producers of high-demand products needed for the war effort. Other factors included overcoming production obstacles; low rate of absenteeism; avoidance of work stoppages; maintenance of fair labor standards; training of additional labor forces; effective management; record on accidents, health, sanitation, and plant protection: utilization of subcontracting facilities; cooperation between management and labor as it affected production; and conservation of critical and strategic materials.[96] The award included a pennant for the plant and pins for all employees.

The presentation of the E Award at Exposition Cotton Mills was a formal ceremony with printed invitations and programs, and special envelopes were given to employees with these instructions:

This envelope contains an Army-Navy E Pin. It looks like the picture above.

It will not be yours officially until the presentation takes place on March 16, 1943.

Meanwhile, the Army and Navy have placed it in your trust. Therefore…

[In all caps, bolded red letters]

DO NOT OPEN THIS ENVELOPE UNTIL THE OFFICIAL PRESENTATION IS MADE AT THE CEREMONY

By mid-1943, the government had standardized the ceremonies and limited them to a maximum of thirty minutes. The government officials cut down on expenses and minimized time lost on production by cutting extras such as drinks, dinners, and dances.

Then the speeches began.

Lieutenant Albert S. Lewis of the U.S. Navy said, "You men and women of Exposition Cotton Mills have done a wonderful job. You have done a great service for your country, in particular for the men in the armed forces who are on the firing lines every day fighting for you. These men are depending on you to ensure that they get the supplies essential to the success of their efforts."

Render Callahance Garner, an Exposition Cotton Mills employee, accepted her E Award with these comments: "As long as there is a cry for production and more production, until we can hear the shouts of victory, I feel safe in saying you can depend on us."

Then there was an address by Robert F. Maddox, master of ceremonies:

I dimly remember the International Cotton Exposition of which my father was a Director, and which was held on these ground many years again and from which this company takes its name. This was the first great exposition ever held in the South and its success definitely marked the beginning of the industrial development of the New South, and it especially demonstrated the importance of having the cotton mills conveniently located near the cotton fields, for at that time the New England states dominated the cotton spinning industry.

The organization of the Exposition Cotton Mills in 1882, just 17 years after Atlanta had risen Phoenix-like from the ashes of war, was a typical example of the progressive spirit of her people, and the subscription to 240,000 of capital stock to start this cotton mill by 17 of Atlanta's

Exposition Mills mill floor, 1940s. *Courtesy of Special Collections and Archives, Georgia State University, Atlanta.*

most loyal and civic minded citizens showed their faith in the future of this city and section. Sixty years later their success justifies their faith in Exposition Mills. It is no surprise that the labor of its large number of loyal and patriotic employees and the excellence of their products have won for themselves individually and for their mill the Army-Navy Production Award for Excellence in War Production.

Finally, Colonel R.T. Stevens, chief of clothing textile procurement division office and quartermaster general, commented on the production of sheeting, sateen, and medium fabrics. He said:

When the need for heavy yarn fabrics especially duck, you came to the game early when production was vitally needed.... Three-fourths of production given to war efforts. You actually did what others said could not be done and you did it so well there have never been rejections of Exposition goods by the Quartermaster Corps.

Chapter 17

THE EXPOSITION ENDS

I n an oral history about Exposition Mills, a former worker said, "The companies made good money off those people. They made $18 million when they sold the mill. Who made that money for them? The people who worked there."

He continued to tell how the mill owners were not altruistic in the end. When mills around the country were selling off the mill homes, there were bitter memories:

> *When they sold the houses, they were overpriced. They could have just given the houses away, but in 1965 they just as soon take a bulldozer to them than to give* [them to the workers].
>
> *The company store was not good for some people; you could take your whole pay and at payday, you did not have any money. Sold their soul to company store.... Worked for 10 years and never drew a dime.*[97]

THE BEGINNING OF THE END

The National Recovery Administration (NRA) tried to stimulate the economy by spreading the wealth by manipulating employment hours. This government overreach was part of President Roosevelt's alphabet soup of social programs to get Americans back to work. The idea was to limit workers' hours to boost others' hours. The NRA also gave workers the right to organize.

Employers resented the NRA and found workarounds. Even the workers resented the restrictions and gave the act a new name: No Roosevelt Again. They also gave the NRA another racist acronym not worth repeating. Some workers organized, especially when unions came to town to recruit soldiers. The NRA is said to be blamed for the violent uprising on Labor Day 1934. Thousands of southern cotton millworkers participated in the largest textile strike in American history. Two Fulton mills took part: Fulton Bag and Cotton Mill and Exposition Mills. The New South might have been good for industry, but industry was violently anti-union. Poor wages, unsanitary conditions, dangerous workstations, and child labor pushed some workers toward unions and out on strike.[98]

Clifford Lovins worked at Exposition Mills beginning in 1920, when he was twenty-eight years old, but he started work at a Douglasville mill at ten. He remembered:

> *I saw some in there younger than me. They wasn't doing no hard work, but they was pushing two brooms down the walks, thirty-five cents a day. Well, that was big money then. I come up over here at the Exposition here in Atlanta in 1920 and got a job the twenty-eighth of March. And I went to work for twelve hours and fifteen minutes a night. I worked twenty-four years up there and didn't even know what a vacation was, not a day.*[99]

Katie Lovins, an Exposition worker, was amazed at the mill: "It's really something for someone who's never been in a cotton mill to see it, and to know what they were all about."

She discussed the process. After they cleaned the cotton, they combined the fibers into a single strand through drawing frames. "It was so funny with my children; they called the frames I worked drawing frames. Well, the children couldn't understand that. 'Well, Mother, what do you do? Do you just go in there and draw?'"

Early in the twentieth century, work was not stressful for the operatives. Then things got tougher. Frank Hicks used to work at both Atlanta mills, Fulton Bag and Exposition, and remembered, "When I started work, they didn't have no rules. Any way you could get it done, you'd do it, as long as you didn't get hurt. The fact of the business was, all they wanted you to do is work."

Clifford Lovins added, "And, brother, if you didn't run your job, they'd tell you there was a peg-legged man out there waiting for your job."

The 1920s and 1930s brought more impersonal and scientific management methods to increase production. Managers watched workers and timed their work. They forced operatives to speed up production.

Frank Hicks remembered the changes in production rules: "They got to where they'd have a few rules, you had to do this, and you had to do that. They was wanting to tell you you couldn't go to the restroom but at a certain time. And if you was off a day, you'd have to stay out two days if you didn't have a doctor's certificate showing you was sick."

Katie Lovins said:

> They came in there and wanted people to do more work. I didn't know what it was all about, but I knew that if you run your machines and kept them going, then they'd give you some more, see. And so, if you worked hard and kept that work going, then you got a little more added on to you till you almost got to the place where you had more than you could do.

The NRA demanded eight-hour workdays and removed children from the mills. These and other NRA rules put pressure on the mill managers. They introduced new scientific management methods for productivity that led to what was called "speedups and stretch-outs."

Effie Gray, who worked at Fulton Bag, explained what it was like in most mills: "After they went on eight hours, see, we didn't have no lunch time. And I worked many, many a day and I didn't even have time to eat my lunch, or even time to go to the bathroom."

Calvin Freeman added, "You had to eat on the fly!"

It is no surprise that mill owners hated the unions. Frank Hicks said, "They would not recognize a union. You take Fulton Bag; I heard Norman Elsas, the headman, say, 'I'll tear it down a brick at a time before I'll ever recognize a union.'"

Clifford Lovins told of an experience with his manager:

> The boss come up to me one morning, like an old setting hen come off the nest. He hit me on the back, he says, "Cliff, I want you to tell me which one has got the most power, the union of the Congress or the United States." I says, "Any dumbskulled fellow'd know that the Congress of the United States got more power than the union." He says, "You're fired." "Fired?" "Yeah, because you belong to the union." I says, "Ever who says I belong

to the union lies by the city clock, 'cause I don't belong to it. And that ain't all, I'm not going to join it."

They laid me off; I was off six weeks. But I got laid off for somebody's lie, see. The trouble in them textile plants, the reason why nary one of them never was organized, the people wouldn't stick together. They'd tell you they would, but when it come to a showdown, they wouldn't do it—"Afraid I'll lose my job, and then I can't get one."

The 1934 general textile strike was violent and poorly organized. Nesbitt Spinks was involved in the strike and recalled:

We'd do most of our picketing in the afternoon, when they was changing shifts. Then at certain times there would be big crowds gathered there. So, there was quite a big stir there. I guess this freight train coming in there was the biggest stir that I remember. The railroad was trying to get in there to pull some stuff out and leave some stuff. And they said the railroad was scabbing agin them, you know. We all got up on the track there. There was

Exposition Mills lockout strike, 1946. *LBCB046-097c, Lane Brothers Commercial Photographers Photographic Collection, 1920–76. Photographic Collection, Special Collections and Archives, Georgia State University Library.*

Exposition Cotton Mills, Atlanta, Georgia, strike photographs, April 8, 1946. *LBCE7-041a, Lane Brothers Commercial Photographers Photographic Collection, 1920–76. Photographic Collection, Special Collections and Archives, Georgia State University Library.*

a crowd of people out there, men and women and the best I remember, there might have been a lot of children out there. And the train pulled right up there pretty close and stopped but of course they wouldn't run over us. The polices come out and ordered us off, and we still didn't go. And they brought tear gas out there and shot tear gas into us. And seemed like the train did go in after that. Of course, they made it rough on the people at the cotton mill, any way they could, that come out on strike.[100]

Nanny Washburn began work at eight years old:

I worked the Exposition Cotton Mill. And my sister, she worked there, and she belonged to the union [United Textile Workers of America]. *I wasn't on the picket line but a short time. The day I went is the night I got arrested. We was grabbed by the law, and carried to the police station, as two Red agents. And they got us for insurrection, trying to overthrow the government. We didn't even have a gun, just had a* Daily Worker.

144

Exposition Cotton Mill picketers, 1946. *LBCB046-097b, Lane Brothers Commercial Photographers Photographic Collection, 1920–76. Photographic Collection, Special Collections and Archives, Georgia State University Library.*

Spinks was arrested on the Exposition picket line: "There was a squabble at the gate. There was somebody who was trying to push their way in, and they was forcing their way in. Of course, they got a squabble started, and two or three got cut in the time of it. I got this scar and twenty-seven stitches across the back of my neck. The company fired me during that time, see."

Fulton Bag was the last mill in the Atlanta area to close during the strike. Exposition Mills shut down.

Frank Hicks remembered:

> *I was working at Fulton Bag. Fulton Bag hadn't shut down. Exposition had done shut down. And there was a bunch, oh I guess twenty-five or thirty, from the Exposition come over to my house. Some of them come and said, "What are you going to do?" I said, "I'm going to work. I've got to get my money." It was payday that day. "Well, what's the mill going to do?" I said, "Well, I'll tell you. I believe they're going to shut down."*

They come around and told us, "Now, if the lights flash twice, just top everything off, we'll go out and no trouble." Well, they flashed once. In a few minutes, they flashed again. They all went out at that time.

Calvin Freeman described the scene outside the mill where strikers and non-strikers mixed:

It was pretty rough. People going in and some of them just went on in. They wanted to work, which you couldn't blame them. Actually, I wouldn't have blamed my father if he'd have went back to work, because actually we didn't know what we were striking for. Didn't nobody know halfway what they were doing.

We all stood outside the gates and picketed. We had about three or four gates and they were just filled with people. They'd just be milling around. Some guy had a guitar, and he plays and sing songs. That's what happened when my father got killed. Guy had a harmonica and was up there playing music and we was all sitting on a curb. And the street dead-ended right where this gate was. And this woman, she comes down the street, rolling down the street. She was supposed to make a right-hand turn there instead of turning she went slam into the curb.

The car killed Calvin Freeman's father.

The mills would not tolerate union membership. Clifford Lovins explained:

They culled them out of there one by one. Because it wouldn't do for them to fire them on account of the union. The company could be handled for that. But they'd find something wrong with your work. Didn't have a chance, Then, when you went to another mill, "Well, how come you had to leave the Exposition?" "Oh no, I just got laid off." Well, they'd notify them. And there was a lot of them fellers worked in cotton mills for years that couldn't get another job.

Mill owners suspected Frank Hicks of union activity, and this is what he said happened to him:

I went to go back to work, but my boss man told me I was helping organize because all them people was at my house. Well, I couldn't tell them peoples to go out. Some of them was my kinfolk and some wasn't, but they come over there to see what was going to take place, to see if they shut down. So, they didn't let me go back to work.

Frank Hicks remembered that during World War II, things improved: "During World War II, they paid better wages 10–12 dollars per week." Hicks described the danger on the mill floor and his injury that he sued the company for: "The Floor was slick, and the work is hard." He mentioned arms being caught up in the carding machine. He described how his legs broke when they slid under a machine. Hicks saw people torn to pieces in the mill. He described a work environment filled with lint and smoke. He said, "With lungs full of lint, you will cough yourself to death."

Another worker said he was done with cotton milling when he could no longer breathe. He added, "I don't know how some of those people lived as long as they did."

Frank Hicks summed up cotton mill working:

> *People treated people like dogs. Some people could not take it and knocked the snot out of the bosses.*
>
> *Bosses would smart off on you and tell you what he could do to you. They just wanted you to work…any way you could get it done.…But as time went on they got rules.…If you run your job and kept it up, that is all they care. We did not keep the rules. Couldn't use the restroom at any time you needed. If you were off a day you had to stay out two without doctor's certificate.… But we did not pay attention to that.…They knew when they made them we would not keep them. They would mix you up with rules.…If they caught you sitting around, you got more work…had to keep moving.*[101]

These workers could finally rest. Those interviewed by historian Clifford Kuhn all passed away within years of these interviews: William Frank Hickes (1904–1986), Clifford R. Lovins (1903–1986), and Katie Lovins (1910–1996). Thanks to the work of this late historian, Kuhn, the legacy of these laborers is preserved. Nothing remains of Exposition, but these narratives leave human artifacts of a lost era. This is how we can remember Exposition Mills.

Despite its exciting beginnings, Exposition Mills is the most "lost" of the Fulton County cotton mills. You cannot find Exposition Mills or its village on a map. Mill houses in the area remain, but Exposition Mills and the 1881 Exposition site were paved over for more industry. The original address was 794 West Marietta, but the street names were changed; the original location is approximately 841 Ashby Street NW.

In 1971, Sears Roebuck and Company purchased the thirty-five acres where the mills sat. They demolished the mills and mill housing and built a freight-handling facility and carpet warehouse to serve the Southeast United States. Today, the area is another industrial location in Fulton County.

PART VI

WHITTIER MILLS

Chapter 18

IF THESE BRICKS COULD SPEAK

As I walked into the Whittier Mill Village Park, the rain greeted me. The late summer shower was brief, but it forced me to experience the remains of the carpenter shop with droplets on my camera screen. Looking up at the roofless structure, now a bandstand or open-air picnic pavilion, I realized I was not alone. I shared the space with a fearless squirrel running atop the bricks that remain, which obviously did not see the sign: "Please do not touch the fragile old bricks." They made the remaining bricks before the turn of the twentieth century, and despite the warning, these bricks were firm.

I walked toward the only other remaining structure in Whittier Mill Park, and the sky opened. The rain ceased, and fluffy clouds dotted the powder blue sky. After walking around this tower, all that remains of the Whittier Mill buildings, I sat on a memorial bench and marveled. This tower housed office space and the mill's chemist's lab, as well as the emergency water for fires. Now, loose bricks and random items fill the inside of the caged entryways. On the outside, the mill tower spoke to me.

Sitting in a tree-lined green space, enjoying the carefully manicured bocce ball field, the playground, and the trails, I noticed a bench. Someone had carved the bench with names from the mill's past—not the owners or managers, but the operatives.

I focused on the castle-like tower and what it was saying to me. Those red clay bricks were speaking to me, trying to tell the rest of the story. The story, however, is not a proud one. Strangely, I asked those bricks to let me in on the secret.

Above: If these bricks could speak… Bricks from the Chattahoochee Brick Company were used to build Whittier Mills. *Author's collection*.

Left: Please do not touch the bricks. *Author's collection*.

Whittier Mill tower on an overcast day. *Author's collection.*

Sitting in the middle of the old mill space, now a seventeen-acre city park, I felt the pain of workers toiling all week only to get empty pay envelopes. Weekly pay diminished with tokens for the company store and rent for their rooms. Sometimes the pay envelopes read "NB" for "No Balance." Imagine the dejection of never getting ahead.

But the bricks were saying more.

THE CONNECTION WITH CHATTAHOOCHEE BRICK COMPANY

Whittier Mills was built on property previously owned by the Chattahoochee Brick Company. Convict labor made the bricks and then used those bricks to build the mill.

After the Civil War, state legislatures passed "Black Codes" to imprison African Americans for petty crimes. The intent to was to keep Black people property-less, with few rights. The problem is that the bankrupt states could not afford to house, clothe, and feed all these new convicts. In December 1866, the Georgia General Assembly allowed the government to open the doors of the prisons to private companies to take custody of convicts for free labor. The only stipulation was that the state was relieved of all expenses except salaries for the main principles.

James Warren English moved to Atlanta after the Civil War as a vet. He first worked as a laborer, but he grew rich with perfect opportunities and good timing. He became a politician and got in on the Convict Lease Labor Program. His first company, the Chattahoochee Brick Company, opened in 1885 along the river and near the railroad in a town known as Bolton and then Chattahoochee. English was a powerful politician and an Atlanta mayor. He became an abuser of the Convict Lease Labor Program. The convicts moved into the Chattahoochee camp, built their living quarters, and worked in this torturous brick company. Between 1885 and 1909, the Chattahoochee Brick Company used 175 convicts per month.

The Whittier family of New England came to town for the 1895 Cotton Exposition and opened a cotton mill in Atlanta. The Whittier organization made a deal with the brick company to purchase land and use their workers to make the bricks and build the mill. Whittier Mills opened in January 1896.

According to Douglas Blackmon in his book *Slavery by Another Name*, the brick kilns were so hot that a former guard told investigators he was afraid to go in there with his pistol in his pocket for fear it would go off. The superintendent claimed it was "a little warm" in there. The company doctor, Samuel H. Green, said the kilns were "a Godsend blessing to a syphilitic negro or convict." He also claimed a rheumatic could work in the heat and sweat out the impurities in his blood. In a week, the man would be perfectly well; Green said it was as good as hot springs.

Later, investigators cited the Chattahoochee camp for its filth. Managers would only wash unsanitary bedding and clothing once a year by dipping laundry in the Chattahoochee River. Senator J.R. Stapleton found the dining hall so dirty that he would not feed "a first-class dog" in it. Camp cooks served meat only once a week because the company doctor and the camp superintendent said it caused dysentery in Black people.

Blackmon, in his book, continues to illustrate the cruelty of the Chattahoochee Brick Company. Before a legislative commission investigating in 1908, a white former convict shared this story:

> *Peter Harris said he could not work because of a grossly infected hand;*
> *the camp doctor carved off the affected skin tissue with a surgeon's knife*

Above: Letterhead for Chattahoochee Brick Company with James W. English, president, on the stationery. *Courtesy of Whittier Mill Village Association.*

Left: Chattahoochee Brick Company reward poster for escaped convicts. *Courtesy of Whittier Mill Village Association.*

$250.00 REWARD!

Escaped from our camp on C. R. & C. R. R., the below described convicts of Georgia Penitentiary:

MACK HOLLOWAY, from Chatham County; Crime, cattle stealing; Term, four years; Color, brown; Age, 28 years; Height. 5 feet 9 inches; Weight, 150 lbs, has lost thumb from left hand.

ALPHENS MARTIN, from Liberty County; Crime, murder; Term. life; Color, black; Age, 28 years; Height, 5 feet 10 inches; Weight. 165 pounds; has scar on left cheek.

CALVIN LOCKETT, from Macon County; Crime, burglary; Term, 10 years; Color, black; Age, 15 years; Height, 5 feet 3 inches; Weight, 130 pounds; scar from knife cut on left hand.

SANDY POLITE, from Fulton County. Crime, burglary; Term, 7 years; Color, black; Height, 5 feet 6 inches; Weight, 140 pounds; has lost first joint of thumb from left hand.

HUGH CONLEY, from Rockdale County; Crime, cattle stealing; Term, 2 years; Color, black.

Will pay **FIFTY DOLLARS** each, for the delivery of the men to us in Atlanta, Ga.

Atlanta, Ga.,
March 7th, 1888.

Chattahoochee Brick Co.

and ordered him back to work. Instead, Harris, his hand mangled and bleeding, collapsed after the procedure. The camp boss ordered him dragged into the brickyards.

They took the old negro and told him to take his britches down; he took them down, and they made him get on all fours. I could see that he was a mighty sick man to be whipped. He hit him with twenty-five licks.

Harris couldn't stand up and was thrown into the wagon, "like they would a dead hog and it took him to the field. Still unable to get on his feet, another guard started shouting at him. He never stood and died lying between the rows of cotton."[102]

This barbaric practice of using convict labor finally ended on April 1, 1909. It was not until 2020 that community activists returned the attention of Atlanta to this dark history. The brick company ceased operation at this site in 2011.

On April 3, 2021, the seventy-seven-acre site became the location of the first Sacred Site Ceremony honoring the Chattahoochee Brick Company workers.

Bolton Road paving, 1920s. *Courtesy of Whittier Mill Village Association.*

Convict labor from the Chattahoochee Brick Company building at Whittier Mills, 1896. *Courtesy of Whittier Mill Village Association.*

The Whittier Mill baseball team on a company field in front of the smokestack, 1914. *Courtesy of Whittier Mill Village Association.*

On June 22, 2022, the Conservation Fund purchased the land for about $26 million, with the Kendeda Fund and help from Lincoln Terminal Company's last owner. Community organizers squelched plans to turn this area into another industrial site for a railroad company in northwest Atlanta. Many local citizens, including the neighboring Whittier Mill Village Association, participated in saving this site as a memorial.

At this writing, the Chattahoochee Brick Company site has a cross at the entrance of the overgrown, abandoned location with a few piles of bricks. The area is yet to be developed into a community green space and memorial to the Convict Lease Labor Program victims.

The Beginnings

Helen Whittier came to Atlanta for the 1895 Cotton States and International Exposition. Her family wanted to expand their Lowell, Massachusetts textile mill to the New South. According to newspaper reports, Helen picked the site for her southern mill and even threw the switch to open the mill in 1896. Family members held various positions in Whittier Mills. Her nephew, Walter R.B. Whittier, was placed as the mill manager and stayed until 1936. The actual owners were Paul Butler and other capitalists.

Helen Augusta Whittier (1846–1925) was the first woman to a run a mill in Lowell. She helped start up Whittier Mills in Chattahoochee, Georgia, and served as an officer. *Radcliffe Institute/Harvard University.*

The mill needed a location, so they arranged with the Chattahoochee Brick Company, which sold thirty acres along the river and their manager's brick cottage. The brick company built a forty-thousand-square-foot cotton mill, warehouse, and storehouse. In the deal were thirty frame cottages for the operatives. Chattahoochee Brick received $2,500 in cash and $50,000 in stocks. The convicts working at the brick company would supply the labor to build the mills and houses.

Construction began in May 1895, and the mill opened in less than a year. The total cost was $180,000. The July 1896 edition of the *Atlanta Journal* was subtitled "Quite a Community Itself/The Operatives Colonized in Comfortable Cottages—Built by Capitalists of New England." The newspaper described the village as "picturesque." Further describing the mill village:

> *The houses of the operatives are built around the brow of the hill in a semicircular shape…*[that] *resembles a half-moon.…The greatest number of these houses face the mill and are built of the best material with terraced yards and plenty of green grass, some of the more thrifty of the occupants already having roses planted and growing. Altogether they present an appearance of thrift and care not usually seen among people of this class.*

Now, that was a little condescending. To this day, legacy roses still grow in the community.

Just as Whittier South was whirling, Whittier North in Lowell, Massachusetts, closed in 1901. The Whittier family was not the owners of the mill that held their name, but many family members managed the mill. The most prominent was Walter "Boss" Whittier, who lived in the large brick house named Hedgerows on a nearby hill overlooking the mill village. The mill superintendent, W.H. Salmon, also had a home in the village on a hill. These two homes were heated with steam from the plant.

It Takes the Village

Workers came to Whittier for one-dollar-a-day jobs. They could take the train or trolley, which ran regularly into Chattahoochee station, to work, or they could rent a mill village home. Houses rented by the room. Most of the homes were duplexes with locks on both sides of all the doors, so they could configure the building according to family size. For a long time, a room cost $0.50 per room, $1.50 per week or $6.00 per four-week month. The rent included utilities and building maintenance. Residents painted their houses and cut their own grass.

Other benefits of the Whittier Mill Village were the company store and a school that also served as a church. Across the street from the company store was what the community called "The Ark." This long building still exists and survives in the residents' memories. The Ark had a barbershop, a shoe shop, a pharmacy, and men's showers.

It is interesting to drive through the mill village today and see the unusual construction, especially the roofs' pitch. New England houses have steeply pitched roofs for the mounds of snow to slide off. Georgia seldom has piles of snow on the roofs. So, when the mill expanded in 1926 with new house designs, they were without steep New England roofs. The older homes had wells and community washing areas, but the new houses had running water. A golf course for the residents and mill managers was an unusual addition to a mill village. No other mill village in North Georgia or Fulton County sported a golf course for its operatives. Workers and managers shared the course on days off.

In 1910, W.R.B. Whittier asked the Atlanta Sheltering Arms Association of Day Nurseries to establish a settlement house in the village. The settlement house movement was a social reform movement that began in the 1880s and ended in the 1920s. Helping the working poor in urban areas was the original intent. The settlement house in the Whittier Mill Village was a two-story building with a kindergarten, a free clinic with a doctor, night classes for adults, boys' and girls' clubs, and social workers for families. The Whittier Settlement House sat on a hill overlooking the mill village. In 1926, when the movement had waned, the settlement house was closed and reconfigured for more housing.

It was not all fun and games in the old mill village. A millworker's life was hardscrabble, especially in the early twentieth century. Life here was still better than farm life, as they had water, electricity, and low-cost housing, but mountain people from Appalachia living on generational farms worked at their own pace. They did not have people standing over them and timing their work and pushing them to work harder and faster. This nonstop pressure is more complex than working for yourself as a subsistence farmer.

Workers lived in mill housing with rules to follow. And if they threatened to strike or lost their jobs, they were out on the street. The mill owners did not design the pay system to help mill operatives get ahead; they were subsistence workers and were tied to the debt they accrued at the mill store. Just as the old country song says, "I sold my soul to the company store."

This kind of pressure encouraged drinking and wild living. In 1905, a group of Whittier Village boys assaulted two young girls in the street. Maybe this and other incidents encouraged Boss Whittier to establish the settlement house to solve these new social issues.

Not All Were Child Laborers

After President Franklin Delano Roosevelt's New Deal invaded the industry, child labor disappeared. Workers had to be sixteen years old to work in the mills. Still, many young men wanted to drop out of school to put cash in their pockets. J. Slater Baker wrote in his 2011 memoir, *The Chattahoochee Boys*, about the summer he decided it was time to quit school. (Chattahoochee was the original name of the Whittier Mill Village.)

At sixteen, Baker decided he would follow the other guys in the village and quit school. He saw them buying cars and boats. Money was scarce—unless you had a job. So he told his parents he would not be going back to school in the fall. His parents had gone only through to the eighth grade, so they asked him if he was sure he wanted to quit school to work in the mill.

In July when Baker turned sixteen, his father told him of an opening in the mill. The second-shift job was filling batteries on the large looms. Batteries on a loom were rows of thread bobbins that fed the loom. Filling batteries meant filling empty bobbins with full ones. Baker was trained on his first day. Even though his father worked in the mill, he had never been in the weaving room. The noise shocked Baker. It was so loud his trainer had to get close to his ear and yell. The heat sapped him.

They introduced him to the battery. Baker described it as "the large metal wheel that held twenty spools of thread, as one spool emptied it dropped into the shuttle and the weaving continued without a stop."[103]

Baker had to stand before twelve looms and make sure he did not let the battery run out of thread spools. If that happened, it would shut down the loom; if this happened, he would face the weaver, who would lose money, and it would take an hour to start the loom again.

He worked with a woman weaver who was tough. Baker recounted, "She had been known to beat up her husband on several occasions." It was not as easy as he thought. By the time he got to loom number twelve, number one was about to empty its last spool. He had to race with a heavy cart and fill each vacant slot. Over and over, he filled the batteries until 11:30 p.m. He cut his hands on the razor-sharp battery head. Each day, his body rebelled. He broke out in a rash on day three, and on Saturday, his wool baseball uniform caused him to pass out with heat stroke. He dreaded Monday.

He did not let on to his father as he forced himself to work every day that week. After three weeks with a little money in his pocket, Baker wondered if it was worth it. He thought hard about if he wanted this for his future. He even thought about joining the navy to save face and quit the mill. At the end of the third week, his boss came up and told him that the man he was replacing was coming back to work. He thanked Baker and let him go. Baker tried to act disappointed and appreciative. On the way home, he saw the boss talking to his father. They were laughing.

The next morning, he got up and heard his parents talking in the kitchen:

> *I heard Mama ask Daddy if he thought it worked. He replied that he was sure it did. It suddenly hit me that I had been had. Dady had talked his boss into letting me work to get an idea of how hard it was in the mill in order to keep me from quitting school. And it worked. When I confronted him about his scheme, he would not answer me. He just grinned. I never mentioning quitting school again. When Mama asked me what I was going to do with the money I had earned, I told her I was going to buy me some school clothes.*[104]

Baker described the mill village as a good place to grow up in the 1940s and 1950s. Everything was in walking distance. They had three grocery stores, two clothing stores and a drugstore. The village had three doctors and a dentist. They even had two auto service stations and a repair shop.

They had their choice of churches with two Baptist, one Methodist, a Church of God, and Church of the Nazarene. They had a sports complex with playing fields. Unlike any other mill village, Whittier had a golf course that overlooked the Chattahoochee River. School was only fifteen minutes away, and the high school was a twenty-minute walk to public transportation.

Baker was five years old when he moved to Chattahoochee and the mill village. It was the first time his parents were not living with relatives. Baker said, "Mama told me that she was so glad that we finally had a place of our own that she literally cried when we moved into the small apartment."[105]

He said he never knew he was poor. They would congregate on neighborhood porches and feel protected from things in Atlanta until they annexed it into Fulton County. Even as teenagers, they looked at these days as the best of their lives. Even when they were shunned by the surrounding neighborhoods.

Baker met a girl who lived in a different part of town, outside the mill village. He went to pick her up in his daddy's car, and her father met him on the porch. After quizzing him, he asked Baker where his father worked. Baker told him he was a loom fixer in the cotton mill. The man got up and went inside. The girl came out on the porch with tears in her eyes and said that her father "would not let her go out with anyone from a family of lint heads, whom he considered low-class people."[106] Whittier Mill Village was not a wealthy area, but the residents all looked out for each other and shared life.

The community shared washing stations with lines in specified parts of town. They shared outdoor bathrooms or outhouses in the old part of the village, though it was a step up from a traditional hole-in-the-ground system; Whittier had spring-loaded seats with continually flowing water. When you sat down, the water flowed and pushed waste into the Chattahoochee River. Baker said, "Men did not have to worry about putting the seat back down—that was not an option! Some folks bragged they had a 'country modern outhouse.'"[107] Later, when the company built the new village, they installed toilets on the back porches. Villagers no longer had to walk to the communal outhouses.

MILL PRODUCTS

What did the operatives make when they went to work? They produced cotton yarn in assorted sizes to make window cords and soft fine filaments for things like gloves and mittens. Other thicknesses made twine and yarns. One of the proprietary products was yarn-wrapped hoses.

Paul Butler and Nelson Whittier developed a particular use of cotton fiber to make flexible firehoses. They had a monopoly, because of patents, on a circular loom and twister machinery. They developed this before moving to Georgia in 1895. Moving south was for the firehose production.

At the turn of the century, the mill experimented with mineral wool, which we now know as asbestos. They used asbestos for various products, though now we know it is cancer-causing. They sold blue denim to prisons in the late 1920s. During World War II, the mill made cloth for sandbags. Whittier Mills has produced garden hoses, synthetic cloth, and even corduroy.

In September 1926, the trade journal *Cotton* reported that the Silver Lake Company had applied for a charter to produce cordage at Whittier Mills. This mill expansion by sixty-five thousand square feet required more homes in the village.

Whittier Mill's monopoly on firehose fabric was lost when a key employee took a sample and his experience to other mills, spreading it to two other manufacturers. Now there was competition for the firehose business. The

The inside of Whittier Mill in operation. *Courtesy of Whittier Mill Village Association.*

mill's expansion ceased. Strikes and other labor issues were the first stages of mill failure.

According to the official history from the Whittier Mill Village Association,

After the 1934 strikes "Boss" Whittier left and J.J. Scott of Scottdale Mills near Decatur became general manager. Scott divided his time between his own mills and their competition at Whittier Mills in the town of Chattahoochee. Scott put the mill back into the black and in 1936 placed Hanford Sams in the manager's position of both his mills. Sams eventually became vice president of the Whittier Mills board of directors under president Scott, who had taken over that position from Sid Whittier in 1936.

Atlanta annexed Chattahoochee into the city. The mills were sold to Scott Dale Industries. The owners began selling the mill houses to tenants starting at $2000. The village changed by extending streets, and several houses were moved to the old baseball fields to create equal lot sizes.

The same thing that killed the textile industry all over the South closed Whittier Mills in 1971. The company line was "…as the accelerating flood of imports from low-wage countries into our textile market. Added to this problem is the shortage of textile workers in this area."

Whittier Mill baseball team with coach. *Courtesy of Whittier Mill Village Association.*

Whittier Mill store at the turn of the century. *Courtesy of Whittier Mill Village Association.*

Outside the abandoned Whittier Mill. *Courtesy of Whittier Mill Village Association.*

The mill buildings were abandoned, and arsonists did their dirty work. The owners wanted to make the mill site a landfill in the 1980s. Victorian Artifacts, Inc., came in and disassembled and sold off the mill pieces. The massive timbers and the antique bricks were valuable. The original mill tower which housed offices and a water tank for fire protection, remains.[108]

Chapter 19

ELIZABETH

It is one thing to learn about the mills with facts. It is quite another to see it through the eyes of its residents. In the 1990s, Judith Helfand came to Elizabeth Pritchett's front porch in Whittier Mill Village. Helfand was interviewing her for the Uprising of '34 Collection, now housed in the archives of Georgia State University. Pritchett was eighty-two and did not remember when her family came to the mill; she was too young. She said to the interviewer, "You know why I love this place? It's the only place I ever knew. We lived in the country on another man's farm. [It was] not very big, and we had nothing."

Her daddy and her grandfather got jobs at the mill, and they got two rooms. Her mother worked at the mill with her father. While her parents worked, she remembered:

We just stayed at home and did not have anyone to keep us. You did not get into trouble. Everyone looked out for each other.

My grandma, aunt and cousin came to live with us when Momma and Daddy went to work. My grandmother climbed up on the safe to get sugar for my soakie (that's a good ol' brown biscuit soaked in coffee and piled high with sugar; it was good). She fell and broke her hip.

My brother and I ran to the mill and told the watchman to get Momma and Daddy. She never got well. She stayed in bed for a long time and died.

Years later, Momma took me to the mill to get work. I was afraid because it was so loud. I was fourteen and a half. The superintendent suggested I

Elizabeth and Henry Pritchett holding son Thomas, circa 1932. *Courtesy of Whittier Mill Village Association.*

go to work, but I would have had to quit school anyhow; my aunt could not do it all. I retired in '62 but still worked. I worked from '14 until '62.

Regular hands worked eight hours. Went in at 7:00 p.m. and worked until 2:00. They would not let me work eight hours. I had to go to the Atlanta courthouse to get permission to work. Little kids worked in the mill too. Some seven-year-olds.

I was a spinner. It has two sides, spinning frames. They put you on two sides until you could do more. Up to six sides. It got rough later; the last few years, you were running.

Pritchett talked about going to work when she was fourteen, and in 1924, she worked ten-hour days until Roosevelt passed the eight-hour rule.

She commented on some overseers being good but said that they had favorites.

She revealed what it was like living in the mill houses. The interviewer asked her if she could have made it if the company had not provided a home:

No! We paid per room, fifty cents. Some had water; some did not. Some had toilets on the back porch. They did not put bathrooms in all the houses until they were sold.

They had a store that belonged to Whittier Mills. You had a book you could buy on credit. A one-dollar book or two-dollar or five-dollar book. Then got "alco" [or tokens] money. It's made to look like money; it took the place of money. They took it out of your check. Sometimes your check said "NB "("no balance"). It took a lot to feed kids, but we had no water or light bills and drew water out of the river for years. Rent was so low.

Had a bucket in the kitchen at first, then got water in the house. Out of the reservoir. Then the city ran faucets in the yards could drink. Some houses had wells. Did not put city water until later.

The interviewer asked a follow-up question on the empty pay envelopes: "How did you feel when there was an 'NB' on your paycheck?"

"You had to take it and go on."

When they got paid out, they were paid in silver dollars.

Everyone felt like kinfolks. We had a wash place. A wash pot with lines and benches. All the women would meet. We had a good time. You had to rub them [clothes] on a washboard and put water to boil and three rinses. We had to hang clothes out on two big wires, but some time had to wait until the other's clothes dried. Whittier Mills wouldn't let us put lines in the yard. They kept the yard and had hedges on either side.

The interviewer kept trying to steer Elizabeth to the Uprising in 1934 and the strikes. This was the point of the oral history, but she did not want to talk about it. Either it was not a big deal at Whittier or, like many, she just did not want to remember those rough years. Or maybe she just could not remember the details. Elizabeth talked a little about the strikes at Whittier:

At Whittier Mills, some walked the picket line. There were fights. Someone got their throat cut.

Doffers' strike later in the 1940s might have gotten cutthroat.

People would strike for insurance, and we finally got it, but we had to pay it.

I could not work during the strike; I stayed at home. No one could work.

Doffers' strike in the 1940s was for more money. I doubt they got more money.

Whittier boys did not like the strike. Some workers got fired because of the strike. If they lived in houses, they had to leave the houses. Sometimes they fired people and took them back.

Talmadge sent out National Guard or the plant deputized workers.

Doffers struck after '34.

In 1934, the Whittiers were still in town. Mr. Scott took it over after Whittier left. Whittier was here when Roosevelt passed the eight-hour law in '33....They were here. When Mr. Scott, Mr. Will, and Mr. Aubrey were here, they were good to us. They treated us right and did not talk to us hatefully. We just liked them. Then when Mr. Scott died, others took over.

I did not like the new machines. When we were on eight hours, we were expected to produce the same amount as ten hours. The veta system [industrial scientific methods used to speed up production] *was trying to get more work out of you. They would stand behind you with a clock and follow you up and down the alley and count every end. But I would still be working if it was open.*

Elizabeth changed the subject:

This used to be the best place in the world. Still is. I love it.

I had an old maid aunt who stayed with me to take care of my kids. They had a nursery in the mill.

They used to let you go home at 9:30 or 10:00 to nurse, then at dinner time, then at 2:00 p.m. to nurse. Some mills made you take your breast out at the gate to nurse, but not true at Whittier. You even got paid when you went home to nurse.

The interviewer asked her about the social life in the mill village:

You did not have nowhere to do [things]. *Whittier Mill had a ball team. We went to the ballgames. Finally, they got a show up here. You got captolla tokens in the flour to go to the movies.*

Work was so hard then, and I would be so tired. My husband cooked on the days I worked. He did it all except making the biscuits.

If someone drank and stayed out a lot, they would get fired.

Best part of community is that they are good people. When someone got sick, your house was full of people day and night. One big happy family. We were raised together and seemed like we were related.

When we moved to Whittier, they had a cow lot and garden where the brick company was.

We never got holiday benefits…nothing until Mr. Scott. Then you could take a turkey, ham or five dollars. That stopped after he died.

Insurance—they took it out of your paycheck. Did not always have that. Dr. Greer was a good doctor and visited homes. He didn't call; he just came around. You had to pay him.

I do not have a pension. After forty-nine years, it closed down, and I have nothing for retirement, and I feel bad about it. I guess I could have worked somewhere else and had a pension. If I knew then what I know now, I would have gone to another job. I did not think I could work anywhere else with no education. I went to the two-story brick schoolhouse and went to sixth grade. Aunt got sick, and momma had to quit and take care of her. The schoolhouse taught me how to read and write, but not too much. I can't write well because my fingers are crooked. I used bobbins that were three sizes, and I had to work on all of them. Joints hurt now from this work in the mill.

I want to die here.

We bought the house, and they gave us twelve years to pay it off. We paid it off before then.

She reflected on the day the mill closed for good and how people look at the mill village people:

We did not know until the last day that they were closing. It was hard. I just cried. I was raised there. If I had one more day, I would have gotten a pension.

I miss the sounds of the village when the mill was working. I do not hear the mill, just cars going to the mill and changing shifts. They had a whistle at shift change.

Abandoned Whittier Mill after mill closure. *Courtesy of Whittier Mill Village Association.*

I think people looked down on this village. I still believe they look down on us. Some of the best people worked in Whittier Mills. I guess they looked down on you because you have cotton on you. Some people always like to look down on others…it's their problem. I am not ashamed of spending my life here. I am proud. I feel like I am as good to God even without education.[109]

Chapter 20

WHITTIER MILL
VILLAGE ASSOCIATION

W hen searching for lost things, I always find living places full of passionate people who care for their hidden history. Members of the Whittier Mill Village Association do not silo their history and hide it away in a sealed time capsule. They use their history to change the present.

In 1994, the Whittier Mill residents turned the abandoned mill site into something special. With the help of the Trust for Public Land (a national nonprofit land conservation organization), they purchased the property and turned it over to the city as a park. The Whittier Mill Village Association reclaimed the crumbling mill buildings to create the beautiful Whittier Mill Park. They hold events in the old mechanic's shop, now a lighted stage, to bring people into their unique space tucked inside northwest Atlanta. Though the mill park has been a city park since 2003, the association assumes the responsibility of maintenance and further restoration.

According to their website (www.whittiermillvillage.com), "Funds from our annual Parktoberfest festival have helped beautify the 22 acres of green space, restore remaining structures from the turn-of-the-century Whittier Textile Mill, build a Bocce court and provide additions to the children's playground." Families with children and couples with dogs stroll the mill remains on well-maintained walkways. A short hike up a hill takes you to the original homesite of the mill owners. A peaceful area surrounds the Whittier Mill tower, where you can rest and ponder what happened here over a century ago.

Besides its website, the association has a newsletter, promotions, directories, and even T-shirts. So many who collect history are not good sharers; they think they own the history. This is not true of Whittier Mill Village Association. Whittier Mill Village would fade into obscurity without its members' willingness to share. This would be a very short chapter without their contributions to this book. They are also looking to the future.

The Whittier Mill Village Association members are active in the community surrounding their quaint village. One member drove my son and me around to show us the other part of the village, Lowrytown, where some houses are faced with "pebble dash stucco" composed of cinders from the mill boiler. Whittier was green before it was cool. He also showed us the cross at the entrance of the future memorial grounds honoring the injustices at the Chattahoochee Brick Company. This group is active in making this a reality.

They recognize the truth of the history of their mills, the good, the bad, and the ugly. Our guide pointed out that the street in front of the mill used to be called English Street, named after the unscrupulous user of convict labor at the brick company. They have since changed the street name to "Wales" in front of their beautiful green park. When you are in the Atlanta area, drive to Whittier Mill Village; it is a hidden and not so lost place. This tranquil riverside locale will plunge you into our industrial past but keep you in a vibrant yet peaceful present.

PART VII

LOST AND LINGERING LEGACY

Chapter 21

SO WHAT? WHO CARES?

I love TED Talks. I love them so much that I use them to teach with and to change me. They tell me what people are thinking. I love them so much I wrote one and was asked to do one in my hometown of Cartersville, Georgia. I did not do as well as I would have liked; I am not that kind of speaker. But I love what I said, so the text of that talk ends this book. Read "Fill the Room" and maybe look it up online and watch me stumble through it.

The first TED Talk that grabbed me by the throat and became part of my life's philosophy was Simon Sinek's "Start with Why" idea he explained in the TED Talk "How Great Leaders Inspire Action" (youtu.be/qp0HIF3SfI4). He also wrote the book *Start with Why*. I love it because it makes sense and answers the simple question that everyone should answer to find purpose in what they do. He says, "People do not care what you do, they care why you do it." My interpretation of that phrase is, "So what? Who cares?"

Sinek is a major speaker who shared examples of this thesis by using Apple computer. He shows the big "Why?" of Apple. He makes so much sense when he uses Apple to explain this concept:

If Apple were like everyone else, a marketing message from them might sound like this: "We make great computers. They're beautifully designed, simple to use and user friendly. Want to buy one?" "Meh." That's how most of us communicate. That's how most marketing and sales are done, that's how we communicate interpersonally. We say what we do, we say how we're different or better and we expect some sort of a behavior, a purchase, a vote, something like that. Here's our new law firm: We have the best lawyers with the biggest clients, we always perform for our clients. Here's our new car: It gets great gas mileage, it has leather seats. Buy our car. But it's uninspiring.

Sinek completes the thought:

Here's how Apple actually communicates. "Everything we do, we believe in challenging the status quo. We believe in thinking differently. The way we challenge the status quo is by making our products beautifully designed, simple to use and user friendly. We just happen to make great computers. Want to buy one?" Totally different, right?

What is the "why" of this book? Why should we look deep into the shadows of these lost Fulton County mills that no longer produce and have disappeared from the cityscape? We have villages tied to the mills thriving because people cared about the history. But does the interest in this topic stop there? Is this book just for those who live in the mill villages or local historians who already know the stories? Why should anyone care today about dusty tales full of lint?

When the Georgia Writers Association asked me to judge the history division of the Georgia Author of the Year Awards, I was honored because just a few years before, I was the one who managed these awards; now I was a writer and a judge. The topic spread and the quality stirred me. One book grabbed me with the purpose of all this historical research and writing. The winner of the 2021 Georgia Author of the Year was Carole Townsend for *Peachtree Corners, Georgia: The History of an Innovative and Remarkable City, 1777–2020*. This is what I said about this book:

At first glance, Peachtree Corners, Georgia: The History of an Innovative and Remarkable City, 1777–2020, *looks like a beautiful coffee-table book. Open the cover and discover Carole Townsend's skilled history narratives. In the end, comes down to good writing with impeccable research. The opening pages set the tone:*

"What we are at risk of sacrificing with change is our heritage, the history of a place, the land, and her people. Once those treasures are bulldozed and buried under the red Georgia clay, they are lost forever; all that remains are the memories, scattered photographs, and word-of-mouth

accounts of those who walked here before us. Eventually, even those are lost to transition, to carelessness, to fire, to flood, and ultimately to death.

"History books can be dull and data-filled or story-driven and compromise the truth. Townsend strikes the perfect balance."[110]

Considering the important topics covered by all the nominated books, local history of a small town in Georgia may have seemed like an unorthodox choice. The author understood the importance of the history of our past and the legacy it leaves for the future. The footprints of history walk us into the choices we make. History repeats itself. History rhymes. History roots us.

Knowing that people worked in lost mills and sweat their living while brown lint filled their lungs speaks to our current work ethic, or lack thereof. When I think of young adults "quiet quitting" in a post-COVID world, I want them to see how their great-grandmothers worked for pennies on dangerous oily floors to support their families. Some of them were small children with no choice. I want the students I teach, my sons, and my grandchildren to be grateful for what they have and how hard our ancestors had to work just to survive. I do not think we should bring back child laborers or unfair working conditions. I just want them to live in a way that honors the past. Maybe they would look at Labor Day as more than just another holiday and honor our past laborers like we honor our past warriors.

I started a Substack called "Elegies of Lost Things." This digital content's "why?" is to tell lost stories so people will remember. One article I never published; I am not sure why. But as I was writing this chapter, I thought about it and knew why I never published it. Maybe I meant it for this chapter. I was thinking of Labor Day in 2022 and reflecting on all those lost people who worked in Georgia's mills. There is a reason for Labor Day. I wrote this in my Substack on Labor Day 2022:

> *On this Labor Day weekend, I am writing my fourth book,* Lost Mills of Fulton County. *The irony of what I am writing about is not lost on me as I am trying to tell the stories of Fulton County millworkers, mill owners and the mill villages on a weekend focused on workers' contributions.*
>
> *Labor Day became an official holiday on June 28, 1894, when President Grover Cleveland signed it into law. Though the originator of the holiday may be lost to history, many credit labor unions in response to the waste products of the Industrial Revolution. In the last 1800s, workers worked twelve-hour days, seven days a week, and still lived at a subsistence level. Children also worked as young as five years old. The*

work conditions were unsafe and unsanitary. There were riots and strikes, so a workingman's holiday came about when on September 5, 1882, ten thousand workers took unpaid time off to march from city hall to Union Square in Union Square in New York City. This was the first Labor Day parade in America.

On September 3, 2022, we celebrated Labor Day 140 years after the first unauthorized workers' day off. Imagine what these workers would think of the emerging trend or the discussion of "quiet quitting." I know what my father, one of the hardest-working men I ever met, would say about "quiet quitting." He would have turned eighty-six last September 1. I always think it appropriate that Labor Day is near his birthday. Sometimes he had to labor on Labor Day at Transparent Bag Company in Buffalo, New York, or at our 1825 home. He was always remodeling. He was an orphan who joined the navy young and learned a trade. He learned to build things in manufacturing companies. He worked hard, and he expected us to work hard. His term for "quiet quitting" would have been "lazy," "slacker" or other terms of endearment I will not repeat.

"Quiet quitting," a new term that blossomed after the COVID pandemic shutdown, is not new. As Solomon wisely told us, there is nothing new under the sun. The term, which originated in 2019, is defined as staying in your job—mostly remote—but just doing the bare minimum to keep your paycheck while having more time to focus on life outside your job. It is couched as life-work balance bordering on stealing. No longer do workers want to get ahead and move up. This may be the fault of the workplace culture that seldom rewards hard work, but there is a certain pride in doing a good job—knowing you gave it your all, no matter what your supervisor or the organization thinks.

As I write this new book about workers in Fulton Bag and Cotton, Whittier Mills, Exposition Mills, and Roswell Mills, I think about how brutal these men, women, and children were to work as they did. Oscar Elsas, the owner and son of mill founder Jacob Elsas, required workers to sign demanding contracts and work many hours for little pay. Life was so stringent, there were strikes and uprisings. Maybe that was "quiet quitting" at the turn of the twentieth century. If you did not sign the contract and the industrial spies discovered you colluding with the unions, their "quiet quitting" would lead to "quiet firing."

The reason Labor Day was established was to honor the early hardworking Americans who were never paid their worth. Today, just driving into the office seems to be a struggle for this post-COVID nation.

Refusing to go above and beyond what you are paid to do says something about your character. Maybe we have lost our pride in doing a good job just for the sake of good work. Where is the pride? There have always been disengaged workers and shirkers. We did not have a fancy euphemism for laziness.

I am excited to finish this book about the hardworking mill workers in the Fulton County mills. I hope you will read it when it comes out and see how far we have come in the treatment of laborers. Maybe see how much has been lost in the value of work.

Chapter 22

FILL THE ROOM

D o you have a dream that haunts you? I do. Beginning when I was an undergraduate—many, many years ago—I dreamed of a dusty attic. In my dream, just getting into that attic was a struggle. For one reason or another, it was hard to reach the elusive attic door. Once it was opened, I was eager to explore that secret place. A long, dim-lit hallway stood before me with several open rooms on either side. Each room was unique, but all were filled with dusty, neglected treasures that I wanted to explore. Just as I began to dig in, it was over—I woke up.

Dream after dream, I struggled to reach the attic door to explore. I would go deeper into the space each time, trying to piece together narratives.

Many years after the dream began, I discovered a new door. I entered the mysterious room in the back at the end of the hall, only to find it desolate. The only thing in the room was a chair and light streaming through a filthy window. No air, no life—the space was empty. No stories, no oral histories, no artifacts, no past, no present, no future. Empty.

For years, the dream confused me, and then it stopped. I stopped having the dream. Because I was living the dream. The metaphor is obvious; this had become my life—finding hidden, lost things and writing about them. Once I could overcome my writing anxiety, I began telling stories—histories of places. Writers and historians know the magic—no, the power of place. Just being in the place allows questions to surface and narratives to form.

The Journey Began in Cassville

For me, this attic journey began while driving through Cassville, Georgia, to take my sons to school. It always felt like something was missing. It was a three-way stop to nowhere. There was something mysterious about this place, and it was daring me to find out more and share its story.

I soon found out that in the 1840s and 1850s, Cassville, that three-way stop to nowhere, was the largest city between Chattanooga and Atlanta. It was the county seat with a courthouse, two colleges, newspapers, theaters, and retail space. That was the start of my first book, *Lost Towns of North Georgia.* I would start with the question, *why?* What happened? Where did those towns go, or why did their purpose change? I discovered mill towns, mine towns, ancient towns, and drowned towns in that book. I wanted to dive deeper into those drowned towns and dig down into the mill towns.

I grew up on Lake Erie. Soon after we married, my Georgia-born husband went to the lake in Buffalo, New York. I remember his strange observation. He told someone, "You can't see the other side." I realized that he had never seen a natural lake because Georgia does not have even one natural lake. He had only seen lakes created by humans. I would go to the human-made lakes of North Georgia and wonder why they existed. I expanded my first book to the drowned towns and came out with a popular book, *Underwater Ghost Towns of North Georgia.* I was not finished looking at unique places, and my search for lost things continued.

Dotted all over Georgia are stoic smokestacks, the remains of textile mills and the surrounding company towns. I wondered what happened to the lost industry and wrote *Lost Mill Towns of North Georgia.*

I was trying to tag all the scattered pieces of history, putting together creative nonfiction narratives, writing the truest sentences I could—pulling out hidden history and lost places from the metaphoric attic before there was nothing left to write about. These stories give our community personality, but they will be buried if we do not find a way to preserve our past.

Progress Can Be a Terrible Thing

I have watched Atlanta creep up I-75 North. I think progress can be suffocating. The Atlanta Regional Commission forecasts the twenty-one-county Atlanta region might add 2.9 million people by 2050, bringing the region's total population to 8.6 million. To put that growth in perspective, it's as if all of metropolitan Denver moves to the Atlanta region over the next thirty years.[111]

What was once "out in the country" is now claustrophobic and suburbanized. Our red clay paradise has already been bulldozed for wider roads, bigger schools and more restaurant chains. It is time to preserve and protect place to salvage our community character—the only thing that puts progress into perspective.

In the 1960s, singer-songwriter Joni Mitchell described what is happening in her folk song "The Big Yellow Taxi":

> Don't it always seem to go
> That you don't know what you got 'til it's gone?
> They paved paradise and put up a parking lot.

I wonder what early Georgia explorers, pioneers, and Native Americans would have thought of this "progress."

In the late 1700s, explorer William Bartram walked across North Georgia. He wrote in *Bartram's Travels* about a place Native Americans called the Enchanted Land. He described a forested land teeming with wild rivers: "This space may be called the hilly country, everywhere fertile and delightful, continually replenished by innumerable rivulets, either coursing about the fragrant hills or springing from the rocky precipices and forming many cascades; the coolness and purity of which waters invigorate the air of this otherwise hot and sultry climate."

But progress demanded those wild rivers be dammed. North Georgia needed cheap power at the turn of the twentieth century, so dam companies began plugging our rivers (or rivulets) to create human-created lakes.

PLACE

Let me pause here to emphasize again the power of place. Place is sacred. We are our surroundings. We are our land. We are our rivers. We are the history of these places.

But we as a generation, as a society and as a people have lost our roots. In the wake of progress, we have allowed our history to be plowed over, drowned, and forgotten. Georgia's history has crumbled into the red dirt and plowed under while we write new narratives. The truth is uprooted and cleared away.

Like the empty room in my dream, there is a vacuum. We are left with nothing to connect us to our past and ground us in our present.

So much of our history is already lost. We have carelessly put away our treasures and hoarded history. Some things have slipped through our hands, and the truth evades us as we depend on Google searches that take us to many falsehoods. We have done a terrible job of preserving our personal histories.

ROOTLESS

Our world today feels rootless. COVID-19, mass shootings, civil unrest…this all contributes to an uprooted society. We have lost our collective community identity. I believe history is how we restore connections. When we learn from our past and open our minds to a slightly different perspective, we can move toward a future that honors differences.

So how do we allow progress but keep our identity? By preserving history. By rescuing hidden history and telling our stories. By filling that empty room. We need to fill the room.

We must go back to the sacred places where history began—and look. Let's go once more to the lake. Lake Allatoona.

ONCE MORE TO THE LAKE

On any day, you will see boaters, swimmers, and people fishing on Lake Allatoona. What most people do not see is what lies beneath. Look closer— careful, do not fall in. As you glide along the green murky yet glass-like water, lean in to see 50, 100, and 150 feet down. You may not know that there were actual communities down there at one time. These are the drowned towns.

When the U.S. Army Corps of Engineers had orders to dam the Etowah River, the towns of Abernathysville, Allatoona, Macedonia, Gladesville, and Etowah disappeared. You may be fishing over Etowah's pre–Civil War industrial town, established by the Iron Man of Georgia, Mark Anthony Cooper.

Cooper brought industry and the railroad to Bartow County, Georgia, in the early 1830s. He was a progressive businessman. His company town, Etowah, was named for the river that ran through it. The company town had iron furnaces, flouring mills, and rolling mills. Besides the workers' homes, there was a store, church, and school—everything a little town needed.

Cooper had it all, but he invested in the Confederacy and lost everything. Then the Union army did its final work and left very little of the former industrial complex and his workers' homes. Glen Holly, the family home, barely survived the war. And Union soldiers filled the cemetery with fallen family members.

In 1941, the U.S. Army Corps of Engineers began preparing the land around the Etowah River for impoundment. While the land was purchased, the corps started dismantling homes and farms for the coming waters. The Cooper family insisted on—and fought for—a new family burial ground before the waters came, burying their past under 150 feet of water close to the Allatoona Dam. A green copper plate at Oak Hill Cemetery in Cartersville, Georgia, tells the rest of the story: "This family cemetery containing eleven graves was removed from Glen Holly in 1949 to permit the construction of Allatoona Dam and Reservoir."

The Coopers filled the room. If not for the Cooper family, who saved everything—every document, artifact, and even slips of paper—we would never know the Coopers or the lost town of Etowah. They filled their room, turned around and gave it to us—to help save our community identity.

HOW TO FILL THE ROOM

In my dream, the empty room compelled me. This was the saddest part of the attic. Nothing was in the room because families ignored their stories. The room is silent because no one bothered to ask questions and record narratives. People trashed their artifacts. History died in this room.

How do we fill the room after years of neglect? Sometimes, it is too late. Fiction writers and folklorists rush in and fill the air with half-truths. We watch these stories riddled with fake news on television programs masquerading as true tales. These stories are more intriguing when we know the whole truth. The facts are much better than fiction.

So, how can we fill the room?

1. Support local history. Help historical societies and historians cultivate our collective community character. Enable the history collectors to make our past open and accessible by making history preservation profitable with your membership, volunteerism, and donations. Appreciate what they have already done and how places are being repurposed to keep history alive.

I love that the Bartow History Museum, located in the old 1869 county courthouse, has the wood flooring from the Lindale Mill in Rome, Georgia. So many of our historic textile mills that employed our people caved in before they were salvaged. Yet many have been preserved; Crown Mills in Dalton, Canton Mills in Cherokee County, and Fulton Bag and Cotton in Atlanta have all become housing and retail.

How can we fill the room and make history come alive?

2. Make history immersive and memorable. We understand and participate in history when we feel, touch, see, taste, and smell it. Recently, I took my four-year-old granddaughter Josie to a planetarium. We experienced so much more than a star show.

They began playing a movie about how volcanoes formed the earth. The theater filled with sights and sounds of violent volcanoes, and we almost felt the heat. Josie is a sensitive soul, and I was worried she would have a meltdown. Fearing sensory overload, I was ready to leave and asked her if she was ready to go. "No, Mimi, no!"

One part fear and the other part nonstop excitement, Josie just started talking. She was performing a director's cut—underscoring the action, commenting on the erupting volcanoes, and experiencing it all deeply. I know she will never forget it.

I challenge game designers and technical people to work with scholars and scribes to create an immersive history experience using all the senses. Collaborate to create an unforgettable sensory experience.

Imagine stopping at Coopers Furnace Day area at the remains of the lost town of Etowah. Scan a QR code or put on Augmented Reality goggles and meet the Cooper family in their hometown of Etowah. Then watch the workers pour iron pots and pans and see flouring mills grinding out meals. At the end of your virtual visit, Mark Anthony Cooper invites you into his home, Glen Holly, and offers a cup, and you can almost taste the wine they made on site. It could happen here. Technology is here; we just need to harness it to help us understand the *why* of our past to ground us in the future.

3. Finally, fill the room by telling your story. Create multimedia records of your family stories—oral histories, YouTube interviews. Tell it, sing it, draw it, produce it, or give your accounts to a good storyteller so he or she can tell it for you. As a researcher, I find that so much is missing that could answer questions if people had told their stories.

I am looking forward to that final dream. I want to go back to the attic, sling open the door, and find each artifact tagged with its proper story, a room full of narrative rooting us to the past. The most exciting thing to see will be finding that empty room full of history—stories about people, places, and things just sitting there ready for someone to breathe life into the emptiness and help us understand who we are and where we came from.

Would that work here? Would that work wherever you are? Start with you.

Maya Angelou said, "There is no greater agony than bearing an untold story inside you."

I say, "There is no greater tragedy than allowing your story to die with you."

Tell your story.

Tedx Talk, August 20, 2022
Savoy Auto Museum, Cartersville, Georgia

Notes

Preface

1. Golley, "Piedmont Geographic Region."
2. Hall et al., *Like a Family*.

Introduction

3. Severance, *Official Guide to Atlanta*.
4. Ibid.
5. Ibid.

Chapter 1

6. Federal Writers' Project, part 4, Garey-Jones.
7. Ibid.
8. Brown, *Slave Life in Georgia*.
9. Ayers, *New History of the American South*.
10. Ibid.
11. Atkinson, *Cheap Cotton by Free Labor*.
12. Ayers, *New History of the American South*.

Chapter 2

13. Notes from the Frontier, "Inventions by Women."
14. Ibid.

15. Ayers, *New History of the American South.*
16. Ibid.
17. Ibid.
18. Trimble and Brown, "Soil Erosion."
19. New Georgia Encyclopedia, "Boll Weevil."
20. "Cotton," *Extension.*
21. Georgia Cotton Commission, "Cotton from Field to Fabric."

Chapter 3

22. Russell, *Lost Towns of North Georgia.*
23. Russell, *Lost Mill Towns of North Georgia.*

Chapter 4

24. Bell, *Major Butler's Legacy.*
25. Petite, *The Women Will Howl.*
26. Bell, *Major Butler's Legacy,* 177.
27. Petite, *The Women Will Howl,* 28.
28. Ibid., 30.
29. Roswell Women.

Chapter 5

30. Civil War Picket, "Kenner Garrard."
31. Petite, *The Women Will Howl.*
32. Woodworth to his mother, letter transcribed from handwritten note.
33. Garrard, "Sketch of Vicinity of 2 Cav. Div. Camp."
34. Petite, *The Women Will Howl.*
35. National Archives.
36. Civil War Picket, "Kenner Garrard."
37. Rylands, "Long Walk Home"; Hitt, *Charged with Treason*; Dillman, "Deportation of Roswell Mill Women."
38. Martin, "Mill Women and Children of Roswell Uprooted."
39. Digital Library of Georgia, "Roswell Mill Women Monument."

Chapter 6

40. Barrington S. King to Catharine Nephew King, 1864.
41. Anne Smith to William Smith on September 9, 1864.

42. Barrington King to Archibald Smith, September 1862.

43. Minutes of Stockholders' Meetings, July 19, 1865.

44. Petite, *The Women Will Howl*.

45. Ibid., 218.

46. U.S. National Park Service, "Morgan Falls Dam."

47. Petite, *The Women Will Howl*, 218.

48. *Atlanta Constitution*, "Roswell Mills Bring $800,000."

49. *Atlanta Constitution*, "$400,000 Blaze Guts Historic Roswell Mill."

50. MacDonald, "Roswell's History to Come Out from Underbrush."

51. Northam, "Northside Roswell."

Chapter 7

52. Clark, *Birth of a New South*, 45.

53. Ibid.

54. Beckert, "War Reverberates around the World," 243.

55. Clark, *Birth of a New South*, 45.

56. Ibid., 49.

57. Stirgus, "Georgia State Students Demand."

58. Russell, *Lost Mill Towns of North Georgia*.

Chapter 8

59. Reynolds, "Letters from People."

60. Clark, *Birth of a New South*, 49.

61. Prince, "Rebel Yell for Yankee Doodle"; Martin, *Atlanta and Its Builders*; Newman, "Cotton Expositions in Atlanta."

62. Newman, "Cotton Expositions in Atlanta."

Chapter 9

63. Cater, *Regenerating Dixie*.

64. Ibid.

Chapter 10

65. Cooper, *Cotton States and International Exposition*.

66. Cater, *Regenerating Dixie*.

67. Cooper, *Cotton States and International Exposition*.

Chapter 11

68. *Masterful Builder*.
69. Kuhn, *Contesting the New South Order*, 8.
70. Biographical data of Jacob Elsas, 1924, unpublished.

Chapter 12

71. Beatty, *Celebrating Its 75th Anniversary Fulton Bag and Cotton Mills*.
72. Kuhn, *Contesting the New South Order*, 45.
73. Ibid., 64.
74. Ibid., 65.
75. Ibid.
76. Ibid., 59.
77. Ibid., 75.
78. Ibid., 81.
79. Fink, *Fulton Bag and Cotton Mills Strike*, 25.
80. Ibid., 64.

Chapter 13

81. Harte, "Tale of 3 Strikes."
82. Fink, *Fulton Bag and Cotton Mills Strike*, 46–47.
83. Ibid.
84. Kuhn, *Contesting the New South Order*, ch. 4, "Causes and Commencement."
85. Fink, *Fulton Bag and Cotton Mills Strike*, 154.
86. Ibid., 155.
87. Georgia Journeys, "Martial Law in Georgia."
88. Jacobs, "Uprising of '34 Collection."

Chapter 14

89. Kuhn, *Living Atlanta*.
90. Brookshire, "Uprising of '34 Collection."

Chapter 16

91. Ibid., 43.
92. Ibid., 217.
93. *Exposition*, "1925 Exposition Mills Band."

94. *Exposition* 111, vol. 16 (May 1952).
95. *Exposition* 9, vol. 5 (February 12, 1943).
96. New-York Historical Society, "'E' for Excellence during WWII," January 13, 2021, www.nyhistory.org/blogs/e-for-excellence-during-wwii.

Chapter 17

97. Kuhn, *Living Atlanta*.
98. Ibid., 212.
99. Ibid., 211–12.
100. Ibid., 218.
101. Ibid.

Chapter 18

102. Berry, "Free Labor He Found Unsatisfactory"; Blackmon, *Slavery by Another Name*.
103. Baker, *Chattahoochee Boys*, 117.
104. Ibid., 120.
105. Ibid., 2
106. Ibid., 97.
107. Ibid., 15.
108. Rooney, interview.

Chapter 19

109. Pritchett, "Elizabeth Pritchett Interview."

Chapter 21

110. Russell, "2022 Judges' Statements."

Chapter 22

111. Atlanta Regional Commission, "Population & Employment Forecasts," atlantaregional.org/atlanta-region/population-employment-forecasts/#:~:text=Forecast%20Highlights,over%20the%20next%2030%20years.

Bibliography

Abkowitz, Alyssa. "Cover Story: Whittier Mill Village." Creative Loafing. Last modified March 16, 2005. creativeloafing.com/content-185002-cover-story-whittier-mill-village.

"Activity: Who Invented the Cotton Gin?" Smithsonian's History Explorer, the Lemelson Centre for the Study of Invention and Innovation, National Museum of American History. Last modified 1998. historyexplorer.si.edu/sites/default/files/Content/Who%20Invented%20the%20Cotton%20Gin.pdf.

Andrews, Mildred G. *The Men and the Mills: A History of the Southern Textile Industry*. Macon, GA: Mercer University Press, 1987.

Atkinson, Edward. *Cheap Cotton by Free Labor*. Boston: A. Williams and Co., 1861. lccn.loc.gov/01031939.

Atlanta Constitution. "The Exposition Opens: And the New Era Dawns Upon the South." n.d., 6–7.

———. "$400,000 Blaze Guts Historic Roswell Mill." June 13, 1926.

———. "Georgia's Spindles and the Music They Make as They Whirl." January 31, 1883, 5.

———. "Laurel Mills Suit Against Power Co. Comes Up." Thursday, March 19, 1919, 7.

———. "Letter to the Public from Fulton Bag." June 3, 1914, 3.

———. "The Manufacture of Woolen Goods as Carried on at Roswell, Ga." By the Laurel Mills Manufacturing Co. November 9, 1902, 1.

———. "Martial Law in Force in Georgia Strike Zones." September 18, 1934.

———. "National Guard Is Sent to Rome to Quell Strife." October 3, 1934, 1.

———. "National Guardsmen on Move throughout Georgia as Mill Owners Prepare to Defy Textile Strike: Situation Tense as Troups March to Danger Zones." September 17, 1934, 1.

————. "$152,000 Damages from Flooding Due to the Morgan Falls Dam." March 19, 1999.

————. "Petition to Incorporate 'The Exposition Cotton Mills.'" March 4, 1882.

————. "Progressive Roswell: Something about the Ohatta Boochee Factory Town." August 28, 1890, 2.

————. "The Roswell Manufacturing Company Is a Most Valuable and Important Asset to the Small City of Roswell." July 22, 1917, E8.

————. "The Roswell Manufacturing Company, Manufacturers of Shirting, Sheeting, Yarns and Warps." November 9, 1902, A1.

————. "Roswell Mills Bring $800,000." February 21, 1920, 9.

————. "Roswell's History to Come Out from Underbrush." March 4, 1920.

————. "Sale of the Exposition Buildings: The Property Sold at Private Sale." January 10, 1882, 8.

————. "Textile Worker Recalls Strike Episode of 1934." July 4, 1946, 9.

Atlanta, GA. "Whittier Mill." Last modified October 28, 1994. www.atlantaga. gov/government/departments/city-planning/office-of-design/urban-design-commission/whittier-mill.

Atlanta History Center Bulletin. "Atlanta History: A Journal of Georgia and the South." album.atlantahistorycenter.com/digital/collection/AHBull/id/18408/rec/4.

Atlanta Journal. "10,000 Spindles Whirling Here." July 18, 1896.

Atlanta's Upper West Side. "Whittier Mill History." www.atlantasupperwestside. com/Site/WhittierMillHistory.html.

Atlanta Time Machine. www.Atlantatimemachine.com.

Atlanta Time Machine. "Cabbagetown #4." www.atlantatimemachine.com/misc/cabbage4.htm.

Ayers, Edward L. *A New History of the American South.* Chantilly, VA: The Teaching Company, 2018.

Baker, J.S. *The Chattahoochee Boys.* Scotts Valley, CA: Createspace Independent Pub., 2011.

Baker, Richard B. "From the Field to the Classroom: The Boll Weevil's Impact on Education in Rural Georgia." *Journal of Economic History* 75, no. 4 (2015): 1128–60. doi:10.1017/s0022050715001515.

B&E Roberts Photo. "Whittier Mills—Atlanta GA." Last modified 2014. www.be-roberts.com/se/ruins/whit/whit.htm.

Beatty, R.T. *Celebrating Its 75th Anniversary Fulton Bag and Cotton Mills: A Pioneer Atlanta Industry.* August 1945.

Beckert, Sven. "A War Reverberates around the World." In *Empire of Cotton: A Global History,* 243. New York: Vintage, 2014.

Bell, Malcolm, Jr. *Major Butler's Legacy: Five Generations of a Slaveholding Family.* Athens: University of Georgia Press, 2004.

Berry, David C. "Free Labor He Found Unsatisfactory: James W. English and Convict Lease Labor at the Chattahoochee Brick Company." Master's thesis, Georgia State University, 1991. scholarworks.gsu.edu/history_theses/144.

Blackmon, Douglas A. *Slavery by Another Name: The Re-Enslavement of Black Americans from the Civil War to World War Two.* London: Icon Books, 2012.

Brooklyn Museum. "Catherine Greene." www.brooklynmuseum.org/eascfa/dinner_party/heritage_floor/catherine_greene.

Brookshire, Joyce. "The Uprising of '34 Collection, Special Collections and Archives, Georgia State University." By George Stoney. Podcast audio. n.d.

Brownell, Blaine A., and David R. Goldfield. *The City in Southern History: The Growth of Urban Civilization in the South.* N.p., 1977.

Brown, J. "Multi-Use Project Is Planned for Roswell's Southern Mill Site." *Atlanta Constitution,* June 7, 1978.

Brown, John. *Slave Life in Georgia: A Narrative of the Life, Sufferings, and Escape of John Brown, a Fugitive Slave, Now in England.* London: Xerox University Microfilms, 1855.

Byerly, Victoria M. *Hard Times Cotton Mill Girls: Personal Histories of Womanhood and Poverty in the South.* Ithaca, NY: Cornell University Press, 1986.

Capelouto, J.D. "Downtown Atlanta Statue of Henry Grady Could Get a New Historical Plaque." AJC. Last modified May 19, 2021. www.ajc.com/news/atlanta-news/downtown-atlanta-statue-of-henry-grady-could-get-a-new-historical-plaque/GDHVRBTAUBCOZDJIZCHWSHLIQE.

Cater, Casey P. *Regenerating Dixie: Electric Energy and the Modern South.* Pittsburgh: University of Pittsburgh Press, 2019.

Chattahoochee Riverway. "Whittier Mill." Last modified February 13, 1998. riverwalkatlanta.org/whittier/index.htm.

Civil War Picket. "Kenner Garrard: Federal Cavalry Leader Had a Big Moment During Atlanta Campaign, but It Was His Subordinates Who Shined the Most." civil-war-picket.blogspot.com/2020/01/spotlight-on-kenner-garrard-federal.html.

Clark, E.C. *The Birth of a New South: Sherman, Grady, and the Making of Atlanta.* Macon, GA: Mercer University Press, 2021.

Clarke, Edward Y. *Atlanta Illustrated: Containing Glances at Its Population, Business, Manufactures, Industries, Institutions, Society, Healthfulness, Architecture, and Advantages Generally with 150 Illustrations.* 3rd ed. London: Jas. P. Harrison & Co., 1881.

Cobb County Times (Marietta, GA). "Roswell Hills Have Striking Past History Factory's Record Goes Back to the Days [Illegible] the." March 4, 1920, 1.

———. "S.C. Firm Buys Majority Stock Roswell Mill New Ours Will Enlarge Factory and Increase." February 26, 1920, 1.

"Collection Space. Jewish Hermitage Museum in Atlanta" | The Breman Museum. www.thebreman.org/CollectionSpace/detail/6f2f6fc8-9857-41f4-b0cf.

Company, Exposition C. *The Exposition Cotton Mills Company, Seventieth Anniversary, 1882–1952*. 1952.

Cook, Ruth B. *North Across the River: A Civil War Trail of Tears*. Birmingham, AL: Crane Hill Pub, 1999.

Cooper, Walter G. "The Cotton States and International Exposition." *Frank Leslie's Popular Monthly*, November 1895. www.google.com/books/edition/Frank_Leslie_s_Popular_Monthly/x7_QAAAAMAAJ?hl=en&gbpv=1&bsq=Georgia.

———. *The Cotton States and International Exposition and South, Illustrated: Including the Official History of the Exposition*. Atlanta: Illustrator Company, 1896. books.google.com/books/about/The_Cotton_States_and_International_Expo.html?id=g8E2AQAAMAAJ.

———. *Official History of Fulton County*. N.p.: Walter W. Brown Publishing Company, 1978. books.google.com/books/about/Official_History_of_Fulton_County.html?id=BU8lAAAAMAAJ.

———. *The Story of Georgia*. New York: American Historical Society, Inc., 1938.

"Cotton. Extension." UGA Cooperative Extension. extension.uga.edu/topic-areas/field-crop-forage-turfgrass-production/cotton.html.

Daniel, Frank. "Back to Days When Cotton Was King." *Atlanta Journal and Constitution*, January 17, 1960, 1C.

Data for Biography of Jacob Elsas. Atlanta: Fulton Bag and Cotton Company, 1929.

"Deportation of Roswell Mill Women." Civil War Talk. Last modified July 13, 2013. civilwartalk.com/threads/deportation-of-roswell-mill-women.24612/page-15.

Digital Library of Georgia. "Roswell Mill Women Monument." dlg.usg.edu/record/nge_ngen_m-2432.

Dillman, Caroline. "Deportation of Roswell Mill Women." New Georgia Encyclopedia. Last modified August 13, 2013. www.georgiaencyclopedia.org/articles/history-archaeology/deportation-of-roswell-mill-women.

Dodge, P.S., ed. *Official Guide to the Cotton States and International Exposition Held at Atlanta, Ga., U.S.A., September 18 to December 31, 1895: Containing a Full Description of the Grounds, Buildings and Notable Exhibits: Also a Brief History of the Origin, Objects and Management of the Exposition…: Issued by Authority of the Cotton States and International Exposition Company*. 2nd ed. Atlanta: Franklin Ptg. & Publishing Co., 1895.

Elsas, Jacob. "Historic Timeline." The Patch Works Art & History Center—History. Preserve. Cabbagetown. Last modified September 28, 2022. thepatchworks.org/fulton-bag-cotton-mills-historic-timeline.

———. Zoom interview, email interview. Atlanta. August 2022.

Elsas, Nina, and Jake Elsas. "How 19th Century European Industrialization Brought Us All to Cabbagetown." The Patch Works Art & History Center—History. Preserve. Cabbagetown. Last modified July 2021. thepatchworks.org/wp-content/uploads/2021/07/The-History-of-Cabbagetown-CHAPTER-FIVE-PAGE-7-20210701.pdf.

————. "In the Beginning There Was." The Patch Works Art & History Center—History. Preserve. Cabbagetown. Last modified March 2021. thepatchworks. org/wp-content/uploads/2021/04/The-History-of-Cabbagetown-CHAPTER-ONE-CN-20210302.pdf.

The Exhibit of the Smithsonian Institution at the Cotton States Exposition, Atlanta, 1895. 1895.

The Exposition. "Cartoon about Use of Cotton in WWII." February 12, 1943.

————. "News Notes from Jefferson Street Church: 'Attend Some Church.'" March 13, 1937.

————. "1925 Exposition Mills Band." 1957.

————. "Presentation of 'E' Pins by Lt. Albert S. Lewis, U.S. Navy." March 16, 1946.

"Exposition Cotton Mills." Westside Atlanta, GA, Marietta Street Artery History 1837–2003. westside.atlbuildings.com/ExCotMills.htm.

Federal Writers' Project. Slave Narrative Project, vol. 4, Georgia, part 1, Adams-Furr. Library of Congress: Federal Writers' Project Mixed Media/Manuscript, 1936. www.loc.gov/item/mesn041.

————. Slave Narrative Project, vol. 4, Georgia, part 2, Garey-Jones. Library of Congress: Federal Writers' Project Mixed Media/Manuscript, 1936. www.loc. gov/item/mesn042.

Fiber & Fabrick. "Whittier Cotton Co. Incorporated in GA with a Capital of $75,000 to Build a Mill in Chattahoochee, an Unincorporated Town outside of ATL." July 6, 1895.

Fink, Gary M. *The Fulton Bag and Cotton Mills Strike of 1914–1915: Espionage, Labor Conflict, and New South Industrial Relations.* Ithaca, NY: Cornell University Press, 1993.

First Baptist Chattahoochee. "Our History." Last modified 2022. www.fbccatl. com/our-history.

Flat Rock Archives. "Large Plantations Where Cotton Is King Was Their Number One Crop." www.flatrockarchives.com/king-cotton.

Flatt, William P. "Agriculture in Georgia." New Georgia Encyclopedia. Last modified February 25, 2022. www.georgiaencyclopedia.org/articles/business-economy/agriculture-in-georgia-overview.

Frank, Daniel. "Roswell Has Past and a Future, Too." *Atlanta Journal and Constitution,* January 17, 1960, 41.

Galenson, Alice. "The Migration of the Cotton Textile Industry from New England to the South, 1880–1930." Dissertations-G, 1985.

Garrard, Kenner. "Sketch of Vicinity of 2 Cav. Div. Camp, the Proposed Camp Is Where the 3 Brig. Now Is." [Roswell, Georgia]. The Library of Congress. Last modified June 1864. www.loc.gov/item/2007626735.

Garrett, Franklin M. *Atlanta and Environs: A Chronicle of Its People and Events, 1820s–1870s.* Athens: University of Georgia Press, 1969.

Garrison, W. "Mystery of the Roswell Women: Fate Unknown after Sherman Sent Them North." *Atlanta Constitution*, December 30, 1984, 1F.

Georgia Archives. "2021 Symposium: From Field to Mill Town: Cotton and Textile Culture in Georgia." YouTube. April 12, 2021. youtu.be/eGvVUyq4_wk.

Georgia Cotton Commission. "Cotton from Field to Fabric." Last modified February 1, 2016. georgiacottoncommission.org.

———. "Live Exploration: Georgia Cotton." 1888 Mills in Griffin, Georgia. Georgia Public Broadcasting. www.gpb.org/education/liveexplorations/cotton.

Georgia Journeys. "Martial Law in Georgia." georgiajourneys.kennesaw.edu/items/show/419.

Georgia Public Broadcasting. "New South | Dreams Never Realized: The Strike of 1914–15." www.gpb.org/georgiastories/stories/dreams_never_realized_the_strike_of_1914-15.

Georgia Tech University Archives. "Fulton Bag and Cotton Mills Digital Collection." exhibit-archive.library.gatech.edu/fulton_bag/browse.html.

Georgia Trend (Atlanta). "How a Yankee Brought Textiles to Georgia." January 1986.

Golley, Frank. "Piedmont Geographic Region." New Georgia Encyclopedia. Last modified August 30, 2021. www.georgiaencyclopedia.org/articles/geography-environment/piedmont-geographic-region.

GPB Education. "Henry Grady: The Spokesman of the South." YouTube. April 15, 2020. www.youtube.com/watch?v=oNeC7i5K5lE.

GSU Library Research Guides at Georgia State University. "Southern Labor Archives: Work N' Progress—Lessons and Stories: Part III: The Southern Textile Industry." Last modified May 29, 2019. research.library.gsu.edu/c.php?g=115684&p=751981.

Hair of the Dawg, the #1 UGA Sports Forum on the Internet. "Georgia Natural Wonder #144: Vickery Creek—Roswell Mill (Part 1)." Last modified April 9, 2020. www.hairofthedawg.net/forum/read.php?8,697195.

Hall, Jacquelyn D., James L. Leloudis, Robert R. Korstad and Mary Murphy. *Like a Family: The Making of a Southern Cotton Mill World*. Chapel Hill: University of North Carolina Press, 2012.

Handbook of the City of Atlanta: A Comprehensive Review of the City's Commercial, Industrial and Residential Conditions. Issued Jointly by the Atlanta City Council and the Atlanta Chamber of Commerce. Atlanta: T.H. Martin and V.V. Bullock, 1898.

Hand, Camp. 2022 Georgia Cotton Production Guide. Athens: UGA Cooperative Extension Annual Publication, 2022. www.ugacotton.com/production-guide.

"Harper's Weekly." V.25 July–Dec. 1881. HathiTrust. Last modified July 1881. babel.hathitrust.org/cgi/pt?id=pst.000020243258.

Harris, Joel C. *Joel Chandler Harris' Life of Henry W. Grady Including His Writings and Speeches: A Memorial Volume*. N.p.: Good Press, 1890.

Harte, Tiffany. "A Tale of 3 Strikes: The Fulton Bag and Cotton Company and the Labor Movement in Atlanta. Atlanta History Center." Last modified May 2, 2022. www.atlantahistorycenter.com/blog/a-tale-of-3-strikes.

Hartshorn, Truman A. *Metropolis in Georgia: Atlanta's Rise as a Major Transaction Center*. N.p., 1976.

Hicks, William F. "Oral History Interview of Frank Hicks." By Clifford M. Kuhn. Podcast audio. January 29, 1979.

Hine, Lewis W. "Dora Stainers and Daughter." LOC.gov. 1914www.loc.gov/item/2018673956.

History of American Women. "Exile of the Roswell Mill Women." Last modified May 10, 2014. www.womenhistoryblog.com/2014/05/exile-of-the-roswell-mill-women.html.

"History of the Bricks." Last modified 2006. www.thebricksroswell.com/history.html.

Hitt, Michael D. *Charged with Treason: Ordeal of 400 Mill Workers During Military Operations in Roswell, Georgia, 1864–1865*. N.p.: Library Research Associates, 1992.

Institute of the Black World 21st Century. "The Infamous Chattahoochee Brick Company: Community Coalition, Faith Leaders to Declare Grounds a Sacred Site." Last modified March 29, 2021. ibw21.org/press-release/chattahoochee-brick-company-community-coalition-faith-leaders-to-declare-sacred-site.

Jacobs, Joseph. "Interview with Joseph Jacobs." By Clifford Kuhn. Special Collections and Archives, Georgia State University Library. Online video and transcript. March 6, 1991. digitalcollections.library.gsu.edu/digital/collection/ggdp/id/5848.

Jones, Hannah E. "Chattahoochee Brick Co. Site Secured, Set to Become Memorial and City Park." SaportaReport. Last modified June 23, 2022. saportareport.com/chattahoochee-brick-co-site-secured/sections/reports/hannah.

Keenan, Sean. "House Envy: This Cabbagetown Condo Offers an Iconic Piece of Atlanta's History and Unrivaled Views of the City—If You Build Up into Its 71-Foot Tower." *Atlanta Magazine*. Last modified July 2, 2020. www.atlantamagazine.com/homeandgarden/house-envy-this-cabbagetown-condo-offers-an-iconic-piece-of-atlantas-history-and-unrivaled-views-of-the-city-if-you-build-up-into-its-71-foot-tower.

King, Barrington S. "Barrington King to Archibald Smith. Letter." September 1862.
———. "Barrington S. King to Catharine Nephew King." N.d.

King, R. "Fate of 400 in Roswell Is Still Unknown: Sherman May Have Exiled Mill Workers 118 Years Ago." *Atlanta Constitution*, July 22, 1982, 119.

Kuhn, Clifford M. *Contesting the New South Order: The 1914–1915 Strike at Atlanta's Fulton Mills*. Chapel Hill: University of North Carolina Press, 2003.
———. *Living Atlanta: An Oral History of the City, 1914–1948*. Athens: University of Georgia Press, 2005.

LCCN Permalink. "LC Catalog—No Connections Available. Frequently Asked Questions." lccn.loc.gov/2007626735.

Leiter, Jeffrey, and Michael Schulman. *Hanging by a Thread: Social Change in Southern Textiles*. Ithaca, NY: Cornell University Press, 2019.

LibGuides at University of Massachusetts–Lowell. "LibGuides: Lowell Stories: Women's History: Helen Augusta Whittier." Last modified August 18, 2022. libguides.uml.edu/c.php?g=1127566&p=8227228.

Library of Congress. "Image 2 of Sanborn Fire Insurance Map from Roswell, Fulton County, Georgia." Last modified August 1911. www.loc.gov/resource/g3924rm.g3924rm_g014961911/?sp=2&st=image&r=-0.103,0.318,1.285,0.824,0.

———. "McPherson Crossing at Roswell" [i.e., Roswell, Georgia July, 1864]. www.loc.gov/resource/g3924r.cws00104/?r=-0.518,-0.066,2.036,1.251,0.

———. "Sanborn Fire Insurance Map from Atlanta, Fulton County, Georgia." Last modified 1886. www.loc.gov/resource/g3924am.g3924am_g013781886/?st=slideshow.

———. "Sanborn Fire Insurance Map from Atlanta, Fulton County, Georgia." Sanborn Map Company, 1886. www.loc.gov/item/sanborn01378_003.

———. "Sanborn Fire Insurance Map from Atlanta, Fulton County, Georgia." Sanborn Map Company, 1892. Last modified 1892. www.loc.gov/resource/g3924am.g3924am_g013781892/?st=slideshow#slide-6.

———. "Sanborn Fire Insurance Map from Atlanta, Fulton County, Georgia." Sanborn Map Company, 1892. Map. www.loc.gov/item/sanborn01378_004.

———. "Sanborn Fire Insurance Map from Atlanta, Fulton County, Georgia." Last modified 1899. www.loc.gov/resource/g3924am.g3924am_g013781899/?st=slideshow#slide-99.

———. "Sanborn Fire Insurance Map from Atlanta, Fulton County, Georgia: 1895 Exposition." Last modified July 1895. www.loc.gov/item/sanborn01378_001.

Longworth, April. "Behind the Strike: How Atlanta Responded to the Investigation of the Fulton Bag and Cotton Mill." *Armstrong Undergraduate Journal of History*. Last modified Summer 2011. archive2.armstrong.edu/archive/Initiatives/history_journal/history_journal_behind_the_strike.html.

MacDonald, Mary. "Roswell's History to Come Out from Underbrush." *Atlanta Journal-Constitution*, May 27, 2008. www.proquest.com/newspapers/roswells-history-come-out-underbrush/docview/337532065/se-2.

Marietta Journal. "Blind Tiger." October 20, 1887.

———. "Roswell, Cobb County GA." June 5, 1871, 0–1.

Martin, Clarece. "The Mill Women and Children of Roswell Uprooted: In 1947, Synthia Catherine Stewart Boyd Recalled How Union Army Captured, Shipped Away Mill Workers." *Atlanta Journal and Constitution*, January 7, 1999.

Martin, Thomas H. *Atlanta and Its Builders: A Comprehensive History of the Gate City of the South*. Atlanta, 1902.

The Masterful Builder. Atlanta: Fulton Bag and Cotton Company, 1912.

McQuigg, Jackson. "Southern Railway Serves the South." Atlanta History Center. Last modified January 6, 2022. www.atlantahistorycenter.com/blog/tsouthern-railway-serves-the-south.

McTyre, Joe, and Rebecca N. Paden. *Historic Roswell, Georgia*. Charleston, SC: Arcadia Publishing, 2001.

National Archives. "Today's Document from the National Archives: Telegram to Lincoln from Sherman on December 22, 1864." Last modified July 15, 2020. www.archives.gov/historical-docs/todays-doc/index.html?dod-date=1222#:~:text=With%20savage%20irony%2C%20Sherman%20invoked,immediately%20publicized%20throughout%20the%20nation.

National Cotton Council. "Field to Fabric." YouTube. August 25, 2015. www.youtube.com/watch?v=0hoHvN289Xs.

National Register of Historic Places. Inventory Nomination Form: Cabbagetown District, Atlanta, United States Department of the Interior National Park Service, 1975.

New Georgia Encyclopedia. "Boll Weevil." Last modified October 12, 2016. www.georgiaencyclopedia.org/articles/business-economy/boll-weevil.

———. "Roswell Mill Women Monument." Last modified May 27, 2021. www.georgiaencyclopedia.org/articles/history-archaeology/deportation-of-roswell-mill-women/m-2432.

Newman, Harvey K. "Cotton Expositions in Atlanta." New Georgia Encyclopedia. Last modified April 16, 2022. www.georgiaencyclopedia.org/articles/history-archaeology/cotton-expositions-in-atlanta/#:~:text=The%20most%20ambitious%20of%20the,the%20nation%20and%20to%20Europe.

New York Times. "The Cotton States and International Exposition to Be Held in Atlanta, Ga., Sept. 18 to Dec. 31, 1895." June 8, 1895, 17.

———. "Mr. Hall Opens Exposition." October 11, 1887.

———. "One of Sherman's Letters: What He Thought of an Attempt to Save a Rebel Firm's Mill." August 5, 1883, 5.

Northam, Mitchell. "Northside Roswell: Roswell Mill Trails Project to Be Finished in November: Work More Than Half Complete on Plan to Add Access Near Site." *Atlanta Journal-Constitution*, September 3, 2018, B3.

Notes from the Frontier. "Inventions by Women (But Men Often Got the Credit!)." Last modified March 24, 2021. www.notesfromthefrontier.com/post/inventions-by-women-but-men-got-the-credit.

Outlook. "The Business World: The Week Cotton Speculation the Chicago Failure." August 15, 1896, 308. www.proquest.com/americanperiodicals/docview/136588329/4C7469419AEE4411PQ/1?accountid=11824.

Owsley, Frank L. *Plain Folk of the Old South*. Baton Rouge: Louisiana State University Press, 2008.

Pandolfi, Keith. "Best Old House Neighborhoods 2011." This Old House. Last modified February 25, 2011. www.thisoldhouse.com/21017798/best-old-house-neighborhoods-2011.

The Patch Works Art & History Center—History. Preserve. Cabbagetown. Audio Interviews. Last modified October 31, 2022. thepatchworks.org/museum/multimedia-galleries/audio-interviews.

———. "Historic Timeline." Last modified August 4, 2022. thepatchworks.org/fulton-bag-cotton-mills-historic-timeline/#:~:text=Historic%20Timeline%20Over%20100%20Years%20Working%20With%20Cotton,times%20before%20the%20factory%20eventually%20shut%20its%20doors%E2%80%A6.

Perdue, Theda. *Race and the Atlanta Cotton States Exposition of 1895*. Athens: University of Georgia Press, 2011.

Petite, Dorothy. "Precious Cargo. Roswell Women." www.roswellwomen.com/Precious-Cargo.html.

———. "Roswell History. Roswell Women." Last modified 2022. www.roswellwomen.com.

Petite, Mary D. *The Women Will Howl: The Union Army Capture of Roswell and New Manchester, Georgia, and the Forced Relocation of Mill Workers*. Jefferson, NC: McFarland, 2015.

Prince, Stephen K. "A Rebel Yell for Yankee Doodle: Selling the New South at the 1881 Atlanta International Cotton Exposition." *Georgia Historical Quarterly* 92, no. 3 (2008): 340–71. ISSN 0016-8297. JSTOR 40585070.

Pritchett, Elizabeth. Elizabeth Pritchett Interview. By Judith Hefand. Podcast audio. 1990. digitalcollections.library.gsu.edu/digital/collection/uprising/id/489.

Reed, Wallace P., ed. *History of Atlanta, Georgia: With Illustrations and Biographical Sketches of Some of Its Prominent Men and Pioneers* (Classic Reprint). Syracuse, NY: D. Mason & Co., 1889.

Reynolds, Frank T. "Letters from People: Colonel B.W. Wrenn." *Atlanta Constitution*, February 9, 1912.

Ritchie, Glen L., Craig W. Bednarz, Philip H. Jost and Steve M. Brown. *Cotton Growth and Development*. Athens: Cooperative Extension Service, University of Georgia College of Agricultural and Environmental Sciences, n.d.

Roberts, Phillip M. "Boll Weevil." New Georgia Encyclopedia. Last modified October 12, 2016. www.georgiaencyclopedia.org/articles/business-economy/boll-weevil.

Rooney, Donald. Personal interview, phone interview and email interview. Atlanta, September 2022.

Roswell Ghost Tour. roswellghosttour.com.

The Roswell Mills. Roswell, GA: Heritage Center at Roswell Visitors Bureau, n.d. Brochure on website.

Roswell Visitors Bureau. "The Heritage Center at Roswell Visitors Bureau." Last modified April 19, 2019. www.visitroswellga.com.

Roswell Women. "Mill Worker Monument." www.roswellwomen.com/Mill-Worker-Monument.html.

Russell, James M. *Atlanta, 1847–1890: City Building in the Old South and the New*. N.p., 1988.

Russell, Lisa M. "Elegies of Lost Things." Last modified 2022. lisamrussell. substack.com.

———. *Lost Mill Towns of North Georgia*. Charleston, SC: Arcadia Publishing, 2020.

———. *Lost Towns of North Georgia*. Charleston, SC: Arcadia Publishing, 2016.

———. "2022 Judges' Statements. Georgia Author of the Year Awards." Last modified June 11, 2022. www.authoroftheyear.org/judgesstatements/2022.

Rydell, Robert W. *All the World's a Fair: Visions of Empire at American International Expositions, 1876–1916*. Chicago: University of Chicago Press, 2013.

Rylands, Traci. "The Long Walk Home: The Story of Adeline Bagley Buice. Adventures in Cemetery Hopping." Last modified October 27, 2018. adventuresincemeteryhopping.com/2013/05/24/1188.

SAH Archipedia. "Fulton Bag and Cotton Mill." Last modified September 24, 2019. sah-archipedia.org/buildings/GA-01-121-0028.

Schlesinger, Arthur M. *The Rise of the City, 1878–1898. Urban Life & Urban Landscape*. N.p., 1999.

Schroder-Lein, Glenna R. "Reviewed Work(s): *Charged with Treason: Ordeal of 400 Mill Workers during Military Operations in Roswell, Georgia, 1864–1865* by Michael D. Hitt." *Georgia Historical Quarterly* 77, no. 3 (Fall 1993): 631–32. www.jstor.org/stable/pdf/40582844.pdf?refreqid=excelsior%3A3ec8f1baf70af6f6d67726cd28bfb680&ab_segments=&origin=&acceptTC=1.

Scott, Carole E., and Richard D. Guynn. "The Disappearance from Georgia of the Farm Union. University of West Georgia." www.westga.edu/~bquest/1997/farmer.html.

Severance, Margaret. *Official Guide to Atlanta, Including Information on the Cotton State and International Exposition*. Atlanta: Foote & Davies Co., 1895.

Sibley, C. "Old Roswell: Town Preserving Past, Besieged by the Present." *Atlanta Constitution*, February 17, 1983, H4.

Signs marking the history of the Roswell Manufacturing Company on the hiking trails along Vickery (Big) Creek.

Sinek, Simon. "How Great Leaders Inspire Action. TED: Ideas Worth Spreading." March 4, 2014. www.ted.com/talks/simon_sinek_how_great_leaders_inspire_action?language=e.

Smith, Anne. "Anne Smith to William Smith on September 9, 1864." Smith papers, September 1864.

Smith, William. "Letter from William Smith to His Mother." September 1864.

Southern Labor Archives. "Interview with Bill Woodam." By George Stoney. The

Uprising of '34 collection, L1995-13. Special Collections and Archives, Georgia State University, Atlanta. Online Audio and Transcript.

———. "Poem Written by a Striker During the Fulton Bag and Cotton Mill Strike." L1985-34. Special Collections and Archives, Georgia State University, Atlanta. digitalcollections.library.gsu.edu/digital/collection/labor/id/4600/rec/51.

Staples, Gracie Bonds. "AJC Exclusive: Will Railroad's Plans Supplant Dreams for Memorial? Slaves Who Worked at Brick Company Are Buried on the Property." *Atlanta Journal-Constitution*, September 10, 2020. www.proquest.com/docview/24 41178575?accountid=11824&forcedol=true.

Statham, Frances P. *The Roswell Women*. Greenwich, CT: Fawcett Books, 1987.

Stevens, Silas C. "Union Private Silas C. Stevens of the Chicago Board of Trade Battery." Chicago History Museum. Last modified July 1864. www.worldcat. org/title/825208413?oclcNum=825208413.

Stirgus, Eric. "Georgia State Students Demand Atlanta Mayor Move Henry Grady Statue." *AJC*. Last modified December 4, 2019. www.ajc.com/news/ local-education/georgia-state-students-demand-atlanta-mayor-move-henry-grady-statue/gaWZYwDGe7bh1r87V8NWlM.

Tanzer, Lynne. "Greetings from Cabbagetown Evolves from Mill Town to Artistic Playground." ARTS ATL. Last modified March 25, 2020. www.artsatl.org/ postcards-from-cabbagetown.

"Testimonials Examination by Mr. Daly. The Fulton Bag & Cotton Mill Strike (1914–1915)." georgialaborstrikes.weebly.com/uploads/4/3/8/0/43801367/ ms004-008.pdf.

Timmons, Greg. "How Slavery Became the Economic Engine of the South." HISTORY. Last modified March 6, 2018. www.history.com/news/slavery-profitable-southern-economy.

Townsend, Carole. *Peachtree Corners, Georgia: The History of an Innovative and Remarkable City, 1777–2020*. N.p., 2021.

Townsend, George A. "Cotton-Growing in the South." *The Chautauquan: A Weekly Newsmagazine* (1880–1914), December 1886.

Trimble, Stanley, and R. Brown. "Soil Erosion." New Georgia Encyclopedia. Last modified July 26, 2017. https://www.georgiaencyclopedia.org/articles/ geography-environment/soil-erosion.

Trocheck, Kathy. "The Old Mill: The Last Whistle Was Four Years Ago but Some Like Aubrey Smith Remember." *Atlanta Constitution*, October 4, 1979, H62.

———. "Roswell Factory Closes Its Doors: Roswell Solicitor May File Criminal Charges." *Atlanta Constitution*, July 10, 1980, H11.

UGA Cotton News. *2022 Georgia Cotton Production Guide*. Cotton Related News and Files from UGA, 2022. www.ugacotton.com/production-guide.

University of Georgia. Cooperative Extension Service. Bulletin—Cooperative Extension Service, University of Georgia, College of Agriculture.

U.S. Army. *Army E Award Exposition Cotton Mills*. Atlanta: U.S. Army/Navy, 1943.

U.S. National Park Service. "Morgan Falls Dam." Last modified February 24, 2021. www.nps.gov/places/morgan-falls-dam.htm.

"Various." *Atlanta History: A Journal of Georgia and the South* 36, no. 4 (Winter 1993). album.atlantahistorycenter.com/digital/collection/AHBull/id/18408/rec/4.

WABE. "How a Mill Settlement in Atlanta Evolved into Modern-Day Cabbagetown." Last modified March 18, 2022. www.wabe.org/how-a-mill-settlement-in-atlanta-evolved-into-modern-day-cabbagetown.

Warrick, Pamela. "Mothers of Invention: Science: Recognition Has Long Proved Elusive for Women Inventors. Catherine Greene Helped Build the Cotton Gin, but Eli Whitney Got the Patent. And Whoever Heard of Hedy Lamarr the Inventor?" *Los Angeles Times*. Last modified September 23, 1992. www.latimes.com/archives/la-xpm-1992-09-23-vw-1156-story.html.

Washington, Booker T. "From the Recording Registry: Booker T. Washington's Atlanta Exposition Speech of 1895." Library of Congress Blogs. Last modified September 18, 2021. blogs.loc.gov/now-see-hear/2021/09/from-the-recording-registry-booker-t-washingtons-atlanta-exposition-speech-of-1895.

Wilde, Robert. "Did Cotton Drive the Industrial Revolution, or Is It More Complicated?" ThoughtCo. Last modified May 5, 2014. www.thoughtco.com/textiles-during-the-industrial-revolution-1221644.

Woodworth, Edwen C. "Letter to His Mother Describing the Burning of Roswell Mills." AHC MSS 645, July 1864.

YouTube. "15 Things You Didn't Know about Cotton." Last modified April 26, 2019. m.youtube.com/watch?v=csdD_T1ctVs.

———. "How Cotton Is Processed in Factories: How It's Made." April 5, 2015. m.youtube.com/watch?v=QHgNoSYlhYs.

ABOUT THE AUTHOR

Lisa M. Russell is a writer, instructor, and academic assistant dean. She writes micro-history books about "lost things." She has guested on several local television/radio programs and podcasts, including the History Channel. She is a speaker and delivered a Ted Talk about historic preservation. Russell earned her master of arts degree in professional writing (MAPW) from Kennesaw State University. In 2020, she received the Distinguished Alumnus Award. Lisa teaches English full time at Georgia Northwestern Technical College and serves as the assistant dean of English. She is a part-time professor of communication at Kennesaw State University. In her spare time, you can find Lisa exploring North Georgia with her micro-historic lens to discover her next "lost story."